EXERCISES TO ACCOMPANY

English
Simplified

EXERCISES TO ACCOMPANY

English Simplified

Blanche Ellsworth

Second Canadian Edition by
Arnold Keller
University of Victoria

HARPERCOLLINS*PUBLISHERS*

Sponsoring Editor: Lucy Rosendahl/Jane Kinney
Project Editor: Susan Goldfarb
Art Direction: Heather A. Ziegler
Text and Cover Design: Brand X Studio
Director of Production: Jeanie Berke
Production Assistant: Paula Keller
Compositor: American–Stratford Graphic Services, Inc.
Printer-Binder: Courier Kendallville, Inc.
Cover Printer: Phoenix Color Corp.

Exercises to Accompany English Simplified, Second Canadian Edition

ISBN 0–06–043646–8

91 92 93 9 8 7 6 5 4 3 2

CONTENTS

Preface vii

Diagnostic Tests
1. Grammar 1
2. Punctuation 4
3. Mechanics, Spelling, Usage 7

Grammar
4. Parts of a Sentence 10
5. Parts of Speech 12
6. Parts of Speech 13
7. Parts of Speech and Their Uses 14
8. Complements 16
9. Complements 17
10. Noun and Pronoun Use 18
11. Noun, Pronoun, and Adjective Use 19
12. Verb Tense 20
13. Verbs—Kind, Voice, and Mood 22
14. Verbals 24
15. Adjectives and Adverbs 25
16. Adjectives and Adverbs 27
17. Pronouns—Kind and Case 28
18. Pronoun Case 29
19. Pronoun Reference 32
20. Phrases 33
21. Verbal Phrases 35
22. Phrases—Review 37
23. Clauses 39
24. Clauses 41
25. Noun and Adjective Clauses 42
26. Adverb Clauses 43
27. Kinds of Sentences 44
28. Agreement—Subject and Verb 46
29. Agreement—Subject and Verb 48
30. Agreement—Pronoun and Antecedent 50
31. Agreement—Review 52
32. Fragments 53
33. Comma Splices and Fused Sentences 55
34. Fragments, Comma Splices, and Fused Sentences 56
35. Sentence Effectiveness 58
36. Parallel Structure 60
37. Parallel Structure 61
38. Placement of Modifiers 62
39. Dangling Modifiers 63
40. Dangling Modifiers 64
41. Review 65

Punctuation
42. The Comma 68
43. The Comma 70
44. The Comma 71
45. The Comma 72
46. The Comma 74
47. The Comma 76
48. The Period, Question Mark, and Exclamation Point 78
49. The Semicolon 79
50. The Semicolon and the Comma 80
51. The Semicolon and the Comma 82
52. The Apostrophe 84
53. The Apostrophe 85
54. The Apostrophe 86
55. Italics 88
56. Quotation Marks 90
57. Quotation Marks 92
58. Italics and Quotation Marks 94
59. The Colon, the Dash, Parentheses, and Brackets 96
60. The Hyphen 98
61. Review 99
62. Review 101

Mechanics
63. Capitals 103
64. Capitals 104
65. Numbers and Abbreviations 105
66. Capitals, Numbers, and Abbreviations 107

Spelling
67. Recognizing Correct Forms 109
68. Correcting Errors 112
69. Correcting Errors 114
70. Words Frequently Misspelled 116

Usage
71. Words Similar in Sound 118
72. Words Similar in Sound 120
73. Word Choice 123
74. Word Choice 125
75. Word Choice 126
76. Word Choice 128
77. Word Choice 130
78. Word Choice 131

Beyond the Sentence
79. Paragraph Development 132
80. Paragraph Development with Specifics 134
81. Paragraph Unity 135
82. Paragraph Coherence—Transitions 136
83. Bibliographic Form 137

Achievement Tests
84. Grammar 138
85. Punctuation 141
86. Mechanics, Spelling, Usage 144
87. Documentation 147

A List of Grammatical Terms 149

Teaching-Learning Aid: Diagraming 151

PREFACE

This second Canadian edition of *Exercises to Accompany English Simplified* preserves the spirit and form of the first one. The exercises continue to offer practice in the comprehensive range of topics that is the hallmark of the *English Simplified* text. However, this latest volume also provides hundreds of new examples and sentences that reflect changing student populations and contemporary Canadian interests. Many exercises also ask students to respond more fully than before; this should help instructors identify what students know and what they don't. Other new features include a brief glossary of terms and a convenient index to the *English Simplified* text; both should make it easier for students to find what they need.

A book like this has two main purposes: to help students become aware of language habits that may limit their performance and, by pinpointing errors, to help students correct them. No workbook can provide enough exercises to neutralize habitual errors; nor can a workbook itself ensure that students will transfer what they learn to their own essays. But a workbook can inform and guide students toward the practice and expectations of educated users of English.

An exercise that lets students guess at the right answer is unlikely to be effective. Throughout this workbook, therefore, we stress the need to know *why* a particular form is correct. Students typically must furnish not only the right answers but also the reasons for their choices. These techniques come from our own experiences in the classroom over more than four decades of teaching at San Francisco State University, Vanier College, and the University of Victoria. Indeed, we have drawn many of the sentences from student papers so as to represent the most frequently made errors.

Blanche Ellsworth
Arnold Keller

1. DIAGNOSTIC TEST: GRAMMAR

Sentences

In the blank after each item,

    write **1** if the boldface expression is **one complete sentence**;
    write **2** if it is a **fragment** (incorrect: less than a complete sentence);
    write **3** if it is a **comma splice** or **fused sentence** (incorrect: two or more sentences written as one; also known as
    a **run-on**).

Example: Trudeau returned from his walk. *Having decided to resign as Prime Minister.*   <u> 2 </u>

1. Sylvia had brought her music. *But no one asked her to sing.*   1. _____

2. Sauvé retired as Governor-General. *Her term in office having been successful.*   2. _____

3. I tried to enter the storeroom. *The door was stuck I could not force it open.*   3. _____

4. The Expos made two big trades after the season had begun. *First for a shortstop and then for a center fielder.*   4. _____

5. The group made Morgan treasurer. *A job that appealed to him.*   5. _____

6. *The weather improved about noon, we went for a walk on the beach.*   6. _____

7. She drove up in a Wombat. *A small foreign car with huge headlights.*   7. _____

8. *Although Corey first had wanted to become a physics major, he finally decided on biology.*   8. _____

9. *The reason for her shyness being that she knew no one at the party except her hostess.*   9. _____

10. *The experiment to produce nuclear fusion was both controversial and exciting, scientists all over the world attempted to duplicate its results.*   10. _____

11. *Moberg learned too late that the typewriter had already been invented.*   11. _____

12. She revealed a surprising knowledge of art. *She said she loved the impressionists, she had studied them in Paris.*   12. _____

13. We walked over to the lost-and-found office. *To see whether the bag had been turned in.*   13. _____

14. *The shift lever must be in neutral only then will the car start.*   14. _____

15. *They were driven back by the flames, they could find no way out.* The end seemed near.   15. _____

16. Alicia did several pictures in watercolors. *A medium which she had never tried before.*   16. _____

17. *If you have a portable electric heater, you may be able to save on heating costs this winter.*   17. _____

Grammar

In the blank after each sentence,

    write **1** if the boldface expression is used **correctly**;
    write **0** if it is used **incorrectly.**

Example: There *is* just three shopping days before Christmas.   <u> 0 </u>

1. The gendarmes assured Robert and *I* that our papers were in order.   1. _____

2. Bill was fired from his new job, *which* made him despondent.   2. _____

3. Each member will be responsible for **their** own transportation. 3. _____

4. There **was** at least two windows in each room. 4. _____

5. Several of **us** newcomers needed a map to find our way around. 5. _____

6. Every MP and senator **was** asked to attend the joint sitting. 6. _____

7. Erma and **myself** decided to go on the tour. 7. _____

8. Surprisingly enough, Smyth was leading **not only** in the cities **but also** in the rural areas. 8. _____

9. In each room **were** a bed, a dresser, and a study table. 9. _____

10. Leave the message with **whoever** answers the phone. 10. _____

11. **Having made no other plans for the evening,** Tony was glad to accept the invitation. 11. _____

12. Everyone in my hometown **was** urged to vote for the school bonds. 12. _____

13. If I **was** queen, you'd be my king. 13. _____

14. I bought one of the bikes that **were** on sale. 14. _____

15. There **were** only eight apartments in the building. 15. _____

16. **Do** either of you have an explanation for this mess? 16. _____

17. The director, as well as the choir members, **has** agreed to appear on television. 17. _____

18. I especially enjoy swimming, hiking in the mountains, and **to ride** horseback. 18. _____

19. Zack, **hoping to impress Tomiko with his knowledge of Japanese cooking,** prepared an elaborate meal. 19. _____

20. **Who** do you think mailed the anonymous letter to the editor? 20. _____

21. Neither the students nor the instructor **knows** where the notice is to be posted. 21. _____

22. Are you sure that it was **him** that you saw last evening? 22. _____

23. Between you and **me,** her account of the robbery sounded rather strange. 23. _____

24. **Hoping to find part-time employment,** I went first to the placement office. 24. _____

25. He joined the Kiwanis Club and coached in minor hockey. **It** was expected of him. 25. _____

26. Given the candidates, it's painfully clear that **us** voters don't have much of a choice. 26. _____

27. I sanded the surface lightly, **like** the instructions said. 27. _____

28. Tension **is when** one experiences nervous strain and anxiety. 28. _____

29. **While carrying my books to the library,** a squirrel darted across my path. 29. _____

30. Norma **only** had one issue left to raise before she could rest her case. 30. _____

31. I had no idea that **my** planning to buy a car would cause such a commotion. 31. _____

32. We didn't think that many of **us** substitutes would get into the game. 32. _____

33. Dr. Hanson gave Karen and **I** permission to write a joint report. 33. _____

34. Although he often spoke harshly to others, his voice sounded **pleasant** to us. 34. _____

35. Neither the librarian nor the students in the reference room **was** aware of the situation. 35. _____

36. Professor Rogers looks very **differently** since he shaved his beard. 36. _____

37. There is no question that it was **she** behind the curtain. 37. _____

38. She had always been more ambitious scholastically than **he.** 38. _____

39. Dr. Smith, together with thirty of his students, **are** going on a field trip. 39. _____

40. Each of the students *were* deserving of an opportunity to run for office. 40. _____

41. *Hilda's* taking a part-time position meant that she had to budget her time carefully. 41. _____

42. *Standing motionless on that windswept, dreary plain,* the rain pelted my face. 42. _____

43. I had agreed to *promptly and without delay* notify them of my decision. 43. _____

44. The dean agreed to award the scholarship to *whomever* the committee selected. 44. _____

45. *Knowing that I should study,* it seemed wise for me not to go to the game. 45. _____

46. *Who* were you trying to find in the auditorium yesterday? 46. _____

47. The noise and the general chaos caused by the alarm *were* disturbing to the visitor. 47. _____

48. As much as I would like to, I'll never be taller than *her.* 48. _____

49. Only one of these stamps *is* of real value. 49. _____

50. The guide showed Carol and *myself* all the main points of interest. 50. _____

2. DIAGNOSTIC TEST: PUNCTUATION

In the blank after each sentence,

> write **1** if the punctuation in brackets is **correct;**
> write **0** if it is **incorrect.**

(Use only one number in each blank.)

Example: Regular exercise and sound nutritional habits[,] are essential for good health.   0

Example: Mr[.] Eliot worked in a bank.   1

1. Modern writers are often directly and profoundly influenced by the past[;] in fact, we can't fully study their work without knowing the traditions they draw on.   1. _____

2. A good horror movie doesn't merely scare us[,] but shows us worlds we never imagined.   2. _____

3. "Why can't a woman be more like a man["?] the chauvinist asked.   3. _____

4. I learned that the newly elected officers were Susie Fong, president[;] Dempsey Lobo, vice-president[;] Sandra Smith, treasurer[;] and Roger Douglas, secretary.   4. _____

5. McLaughlin won on the fourth ballot[. T]he vote for leader having been extremely close.   5. _____

6. The puppy wagged it[']s tail excitedly.   6. _____

7. Eventually, everybody comes to Rick's[;] the best saloon in Casablanca.   7. _____

8. Louise's flight having been announced[,] she hurried to board the plane.   8. _____

9. We had misplaced our road map[,] we did not know which road to take.   9. _____

10. That is not the Sullivans' boat; at least, I think that it isn't their[']s.   10. _____

11. Since you're done reading the comic section[,] please pass it over to me.   11. _____

12. Inspector Trace asked, "Is that all you remember?[" "]Are you sure?"   12. _____

13. "The report is ready," Farnsworth said[,] "I'm sending it to the supervisor today."   13. _____

14. Didn't I hear you say, "I especially like blueberry pie"[?]   14. _____

15. Joe enrolled in a community college[;] although he had planned originally to attend a university.   15. _____

16. Stanley moved to Calgary[,] where he hoped to open a restaurant.   16. _____

17. That was a bit too close for comfort[,] wasn't it?   17. _____

18. The advertiser received more than two[-]hundred replies.   18. _____

19. Agnes is asking for two week[']s vacation to visit relatives in Québec.   19. _____

20. On April 7, 1976[,] the Citizens' Committee held a meeting in the Civic Auditorium.   20. _____

21. The womens['] basketball team has reached the quarter finals.   21. _____

22. I purchased several items[;] such as pencils, paper, a pen, and a notebook.   22. _____

23. She received twenty[-]three greeting cards on her sixtieth birthday.   23. _____

24. He hurried across the campus[,] and up the steps of the library.   24. _____

25. Many weeks before school was out[;] he had applied for a summer job.   25. _____

26. Dear Sir[;] Can you use an extra stock boy in your store this summer?   26. _____

27. Schweitzer summed up his ethics as "reverence for life[,]" a phrase which came to him during his early years in Africa.   27. _____

28. We asked the custodian how many people the auditorium would hold[?]   28. _____

29. "As for who won the election[—]well, not all the votes have been counted," she said.   29. _____

30. Polly asked ["]if I had seen where she had put her glasses.["]   30. _____

31. Any music[,] which is not jazz[,] does not appeal to him.   31. _____

32. "Election results are coming in quickly now," the newscaster announced[;] "and we should be able to predict the winner soon."   32. _____

33. The gates are locked[,] therefore, we shall have to visit the museum some other day.   33. _____

34. The children went to the zoo[;] bought ice-cream cones[;] fed peanuts to the elephants[;] and watched the seals perform their tricks while being fed.   34. _____

35. The camp director said, "The children like to sing ["]For He's a Jolly Good Fellow.["]"   35. _____

36. Eleanor, who is a high-school senior, plans to be a nurse[;] but Adele, who is a college junior, wants to be a doctor.   36. _____

37. *Sesame Street* is produced by the Childrens['] Television Workshop.   37. _____

38. I shall go to the picnic[,] if someone offers me transportation.   38. _____

39. Because he had watched a late show on television[,] he failed to hear his alarm clock.   39. _____

40. Because of showers in the afternoon[,] the game had to be postponed.   40. _____

41. That distinguished gentleman wearing the gray suit[,] has represented us in Parliament for twenty years.   41. _____

42. The scholarship award went to Julia Brown, the student[,] who had the highest grades.   42. _____

43. The custodian was carrying[:] a broom, a dustpan, and a mop.   43. _____

44. Elsie soon found that all the foods[,] which she especially liked[,] were high in calories.   44. _____

45. Esther Greenberg[,] who is my roommate[,] comes from a small town in Saskatchewan.   45. _____

46. "Only two people hav[']ent completed the assignment," the teacher said.   46. _____

47. The talk show host[,] irritated and impatient[,] cut off the caller who insisted he was calling from aboard a flying saucer.   47. _____

48. She went shopping[,] her salary check having arrived in the afternoon mail.   48. _____

49. A note under the door read: "Sorry you weren't in. The Emerson[']s."   49. _____

50. His father wanted him to be a banker[,] he wanted to be a musician or an actor.   50. _____

51. He chopped wood for the fireplace[;] he piled the logs on the hearth.   51. _____

52. The movie did not sell many tickets[.] Because nobody wanted to watch a four-hour documentary about dry cleaning.   52. _____

53. The two boys, not knowing their way in the city[;] asked for directions.   53. _____

54. By saving her money[,] Laura was able to attend college.   54. _____

55. To gain recognition as a speaker[;] he accepted all invitations to appear before civic groups.   55. _____

56. Sue Allen[,] who is a second-year student[,] is president of the Engineering Students' Association.   56. _____

57. Any man[,] who still opens the car door for his date[,] might well be considered old-fashioned.   57. _____

58. "Oh dear[,] I hope I'm not late," said Clarence.   58. _____

59. "Now you have only one guess left!"[,] gloated Rumpelstiltskin.   59. _____

60. While speaking, the club president never knew the moment[,] at which someone might interrupt him.   60. _____

61. We considered going to a movie[,] when our classes were over.   61. _____

62. The church having burned to the ground[,] the villagers undertook plans to replace it.   62. _____

63. I visited a town[,] where my aunt and uncle had once lived.   63. _____

64. She spent the summer in Hawaii[,] where she enjoyed swimming in the surf.   64. _____

65. Having learned that she was eligible for a scholarship[,] she turned in her application.   65. _____

66. The fact that he had not yet found a place to live[,] did not especially bother him.   66. _____

67. Stand with your hips flush against the wall[,] then see how far forward you can bend without losing your balance.   67. _____

3. DIAGNOSTIC TEST: MECHANICS, SPELLING, USAGE

Capitalization

In each blank,

write **1** if the boldface word(s) **follow** the rules of capitalization;
write **0** if they **do not.**

Example: Mazo de la Roche was born in **Newmarket, Ontario.** ___1___

Example: She comes from my **City.** ___0___

1. All **Actors** must attend. 1. _____

2. My **high school** days were fun. 2. _____

3. He attends West Hill **high school.** 3. _____

4. The **Premier** attended the meeting. 4. _____

5. Harry decided to go to work in the **North.** 5. _____

6. She sent her **Mother** a gift. 6. _____

7. I failed **french** again. 7. _____

8. She is in France; **He** is at home. 8. _____

9. "Are you coming?" **she** asked. 9. _____

10. I love **Chinese** food. 10. _____

11. We saluted the **canadian** flag. 11. _____

12. Last **Summer** I worked in a store. 12. _____

13. My birthday was on **Friday.** 13. _____

14. I am enrolled in courses in **philosophy** and French. 14. _____

15. She went **north** for Christmas. 15. _____

16. Please, **Father;** it's early. 16. _____

17. My **Aunt Martha** came to visit. 17. _____

18. "Stop!" **shouted** the officer. 18. _____

19. Roger refused to be **Chairman** of the committee. 19. _____

20. "If possible," he said, **"Come** early." 20. _____

Abbreviations and Numbers

In each blank,

write **1** if the boldface abbreviation or number is used **correctly;**
write **0** if it is used **incorrectly.**

Example: I love **Ont.** ___0___

1. **Six million** people died. 1. _____

2. He is now **9** years old. 2. _____

3. The show starts at **8 P.M.** 3. _____

4. Dana was born on May **1st,** 1970. 4. _____

5. The rent is **$325** a month. 5. _____

6. The interest comes to **12** percent. 6. _____

7. I need to talk to the **prof.** 7. _____

8. There are **nineteen** women in the club. 8. _____

9. **1988** was another bad year for farmers. 9. _____

10. I wrote a note to **Dr.** Levy. 10. _____

11. He works at the Swiss Import **Co.** 11. _____

12. She lives on Buchanan **Ave.** 12. _____

13. We consulted Eric Brown, **Ph.D.** 13. _____

14. Our appointment is at **4** o'clock. 14. _____

15. I slept only **3** hours last night. 15. _____

Spelling

In each sentence, **one** boldface word is **misspelled**; write its number in the blank.

Example: (1)*Its* (2)*too* late (3)*to* go.   <u> 1 </u>

1. It was a (1)*privilege* to visit the (2)*phychology* (3)*professor's* class.   1. _____

2. The (1)*goverment* expert insisted on (2)*repetition* in the (3)*mathematics* class.   2. _____

3. The (1)*mischievous* child became less (2)*aggressive* after attending (3)*kindegarten.*   3. _____

4. She was (1)*optimistic* about the possibility of (2)*competition* in (3)*atheletics.*   4. _____

5. She was (1)*embarrassed* because of (2)*occasionally* writing (3)*mispelled* words.   5. _____

6. Two (1)*laboratory* courses were (2)*reccomended* by the high school (3)*principal.*   6. _____

7. The anthropologist was (1)*sincerely* puzzled when told that the behavior she thought (2)*courteous* was (3)*sacreligious.*   7. _____

8. We decided to test her (1)*intelligence,* (2)*knowledge,* and (3)*persistance.*   8. _____

9. It was impossible to (1)*acommodate* every (2)*conceivable* request, but Margaret took all (3)*necessary* steps to please her guests.   9. _____

10. Because she was (1)*diligent,* she was (2)*dissatisfied* with other than (3)*excellant* grades.   10. _____

11. It's (1)*permissable* to (2)*criticize* such (3)*outrageous* behavior, isn't it?   11. _____

12. The film showed the (1)*wierd* behavior of Count Thrasos, a true (2)*villain* who went to any length to (3)*pursue* evil.   12. _____

13. It was (1)*definite* that he needed to (2)*acquire* a knowledge of (3)*grammer.*   13. _____

14. It had (1)*occurred* to me that the (2)*omission* might weaken our (3)*arguement.*   14. _____

15. It was (1)*apparent* that a (2)*separate* (3)*questionaire* would be necessary.   15. _____

Usage

In the blank after each sentence,

    write **1** if the boldface expression is used **correctly**;
    write **0** if it is used **incorrectly**.

Example: Toronto is the provincial **capitol.**   <u> 0 </u>

1. Hers is different **than** mine.   1. _____

2. Orser was **alright** despite his fall.   2. _____

3. The plane began its **descent** for Newark.   3. _____

4. Audrey complains **considerably.**   4. _____

5. The boxes **lay** where I had put them.   5. _____

6. He was **somewhat** disturbed.   6. _____

7. We didn't play **good** in the last quarter.   7. _____

8. She is not **enthused** about geometry.   8. _____

9. The clock was **lying** on its side.   9. _____

10. No one predicted the **affects** of the bomb.   10. _____

11. He **could scarcely** walk.   11. _____

12. I dislike **those kind** of people.   12. _____

13. We are going to **canvas** money for the Christmas Fund.   13. _____

14. The lamp **sits** on a small table.   14. _____

15. The house was **already** rented.   15. _____

16. The **principal** spoke to the students.   16. _____

17. I **had ought** to learn to drive.   17. _____

18. I stayed **for a while** longer. 18. _____

19. **Almost** everyone had left. 19. _____

20. He made **less** mistakes than I did. 20. _____

21. She **rarely ever** eats candy. 21. _____

22. The package had **burst** open. 22. _____

23. Mrs. Grundy **censured** so much of the play, it was unintelligible. 23. _____

24. I shall not **accept** the offer. 24. _____

25. **Irregardless** of the dense fog, I drove. 25. _____

26. Three provinces **comprise** the Maritimes. 26. _____

27. Data **are** now available. 27. _____

28. **Being that** I was tired, I left. 28. _____

29. I phoned **in regard to** employment. 29. _____

30. I **ought to of** called you. 30. _____

4. GRAMMAR: PARTS OF A SENTENCE

(Study G-1.)

One of the numbers beneath each sentence marks the point where the **complete subject** ends and the **complete predicate** begins. Write that number in the blank.

Example: Dwight's youngest sister was named Lorraine.   2
               1   2   3

1. The Old Port was restored and reopened in 1983.   1. _____
      1   2   3

2. Many of the abandoned railroad stations of America and Canada have been restored for other uses.   2. _____
                                1   2   3

3. Both the Calgary Flames and the Edmonton Oilers made the playoffs in 1989.   3. _____
                          1   2   3

4. The inspired singing of the children's choir filled us with tears of joy.   4. _____
         1   2   3   4

5. Word processors, with their power to make editing easy, allow writers to revise as often as they wish.   5. _____
         1   2   3

6. I have never in my career seen such incompetence.   6. _____
   1   2   3   4

7. Which of the two cars is working today?   7. _____
      1   2 3   4

8. Rarely would she leave her apartment after his death. [*This inverted-word-order sentence, rewritten

   in subject-predicate order, becomes* She would rarely leave her apartment after his death.]   8. _____
                                          1   2   3   4

9. Which of the two cars have you driven today? [*Rewritten in subject-predicate order:* You have driven
                                                                                          1

   which of the two cars today?]   9. _____
      2   3

10. When did the dean and the director of admissions decide on your acceptance? [*Rewritten in

    subject-predicate order:* The dean and the director of admissions did decide on your acceptance
                                1   2   3 4   5

    when?]   10. _____

Write **1** if the boldface word is a **subject** (or part of a compound subject).
Write **2** if it is a **predicate** (verb).
Write **3** if it is a **complement** (or part of a compound complement).
(Use the first column for the first boldface word, the second column for the second.)

Example: *Wendell* played a great *game.*   1   3
             The *crew* of the ship *was* afraid.   1   2

1. *All* perform their tragic *play.*   1. ____ ____

2. Champion athletes *spend* much *time* training and competing.   2. ____ ____

3. *Time* and *tide* wait for no one.   3. ____ ____

4. Not many *ships dock* here lately.   4. ____ ____

5. *We* could see the *caribou* from where we stood.   5. _____ _____

6. The *committee voted* unanimously against the bill.   6. _____ _____

7. The clustered *lights* far below the plane were *cities.*   7. _____ _____

8. A beacon *lights* the *runway* for arriving planes at night.   8. _____ _____

9. Often the consequences of failure in a career are personal *depression* and economic
   hardship.   9. _____ _____

10. *Have you* any plans for the weekend?   10. _____ _____

5. GRAMMAR: PARTS OF SPEECH

(Study G-2. Also study G-3 through G-6.)

Write the number (**1** to **8**, from the list below) of the **part of speech** of each boldface word:

1. noun	3. verb	5. adverb	7. conjunction
2. pronoun	4. adjective	6. preposition	8. interjection

Example: Carmen wrote *poems.*   __1__

1. Molly is a *singer* in a band. 1. _____
2. You must *replace* the alternator. 2. _____
3. *She* invented a better mousetrap. 3. _____
4. The new abortion law affects *all.* 4. _____
5. Robert felt *tired.* 5. _____
6. She was *here* a moment ago. 6. _____
7. The lot sells *new* and used cars. 7. _____
8. The test was hard *but* fair. 8. _____
9. Do you want fries *with* that? 9. _____
10. *This* book is mine. 10. _____
11. *This* is the car to buy. 11. _____
12. She lives *across* the street. 12. _____
13. Is this *your* book? 13. _____
14. The book is *mine.* 14. _____
15. He wants an *education.* 15. _____
16. She looks *like* her mother. 16. _____
17. He agreed to proceed *slowly.* 17. _____
18. They *were sleeping* soundly at noon. 18. _____
19. I found an *unusual* stone. 19. _____
20. She is *unusually* talented. 20. _____
21. *Everyone* joined in the protest. 21. _____
22. The *synagogue* is a landmark. 22. _____
23. Students from all parts of the country *had come* to the memorial. 23. _____
24. The workers took a *strike* vote. 24. _____
25. He is the one *whom* I suspect. 25. _____

26. He whistles *while* he works. 26. _____
27. What is your *plan?* 27. _____
28. Nancy *is* a feminist. 28. _____
29. No one came *after* ten o'clock. 29. _____
30. Put the book *there.* 30. _____
31. I saw him *once.* 31. _____
32. The *theater* was dark. 32. _____
33. He owns a *drugstore.* 33. _____
34. Weren't *you* surprised? 34. _____
35. They waited *for* us. 35. _____
36. The oil spill was very *damaging.* 36. _____
37. Did you pay your *dues?* 37. _____
38. *All* survivors were calm. 38. _____
39. *All* were calm. 39. _____
40. The child slept *quietly.* 40. _____
41. She *became* an executive. 41. _____
42. *Well,* what shall we do now? 42. _____
43. He worked *during* the summer. 43. _____
44. *Tomorrow* is her birthday. 44. _____
45. Will she call *tomorrow?* 45. _____
46. *If* I go, will you come? 46. _____
47. Leo hid *behind* the curtain. 47. _____
48. He *should* never *have been advanced* in rank. 48. _____
49. He drives *fast.* 49. _____
50. Iris arrived at the park *early.* 50. _____

6. GRAMMAR: PARTS OF SPEECH

(Study G-2. Also study G-3 through G-6.)

Write the number (**1** to **8,** from the list below) of the **part of speech** of each boldface word or phrase:

1. noun	3. verb	5. adverb	7. conjunction
2. pronoun	4. adjective	6. preposition	8. interjection

Example: Emilio planned to become a **surgeon.**   _1_

1. **Clarify** what you mean.   1. _____
2. The all-news channel began **today.**   2. _____
3. **What** is the object of the game?   3. _____
4. She **never** confides in anyone.   4. _____
5. **May** I **call** you early on Friday?   5. _____
6. **Stately** trees surrounded the mansion.   6. _____
7. She enjoys tennis **and** boating.   7. _____
8. They **are** business associates.   8. _____
9. **Which** is your locker?   9. _____
10. Write to me **when** you can.   10. _____
11. **He** cannot believe her reply.   11. _____
12. **Neither** of the candidates spoke.   12. _____
13. **The** journey proved quite hazardous.   13. _____
14. The journey proved **quite** hazardous.   14. _____
15. With a few more votes, Hansen **would have been elected.**   15. _____
16. **Ah,** I thought you would agree.   16. _____
17. She spoke with genuine **feeling.**   17. _____
18. Mr. Wilson **is** a licensed pharmacist.   18. _____
19. The jury decided that there was **criminal** intent.   19. _____
20. She **is painting** their house.   20. _____
21. **Maple** trees in Québec are threatened by acid rain.   21. _____
22. He objected **strenuously.**   22. _____
23. This plane goes **to** Regina.   23. _____
24. He is a real **diplomat.**   24. _____
25. **Unless** you qualify, you will be unable to compete.   25. _____
26. Emily stood **motionless.**   26. _____
27. Emily seemed in perpetual **motion.**   27. _____
28. Give the report to either Henry **or** Fred.   28. _____
29. The child was very **irritable.**   29. _____
30. Do you recognize **this** name?   30. _____
31. **Somebody** will surely notify you.   31. _____
32. She lives **on** a ranch in Alberta.   32. _____
33. The motive for the crime will **soon** become clear.   33. _____
34. **This** is a thankless task.   34. _____
35. **Accept** her offer without delay.   35. _____
36. I arrived **too** late to see him.   36. _____
37. Everybody talks **about** the weather.   37. _____
38. The child spoke **hesitantly.**   38. _____
39. You are **now** approaching Paris.   39. _____
40. The car was not new, but **it** was in good condition.   40. _____
41. **Roth** never published a second novel.   41. _____
42. He **has** always **liked** good food.   42. _____
43. We plan to make **an** early start.   43. _____
44. I want an **up-to-date** directory.   44. _____
45. Sit **between** Lois and me.   45. _____
46. The rug **should have been sent** to us three days ago.   46. _____
47. He fell **because** he was dizzy.   47. _____
48. **None** of the students failed.   48. _____
49. Van began to play **beautifully.**   49. _____
50. Supplies were **not** available.   50. _____

7. GRAMMAR: PARTS OF SPEECH AND THEIR USES

(Study G-2 through G-6.)

In the first column, write the number (**1** to **8**, from the list below) of the **part of speech** of each boldface word.
In the second column, write the number (**9** to **25**, from the list) that tells how the word is used:

1. noun	9. subject
	10. direct object
2. pronoun	11. indirect object
	12. subjective complement
	13. objective complement
	14. object of preposition
3. verb	15. predicate
4. adjective	16. modifying noun or pronoun
	17. subjective complement
	18. objective complement
5. adverb	19. modifying verb
	20. modifying adjective
	21. modifying adverb
6. preposition	22. introducing prepositional phrase
7. conjunction	23. coordinating: joining words, phrases, or clauses of equal rank
	24. subordinating: introducing dependent clause
8. interjection	25. showing emotion

	Part of Speech	Use		Part of Speech	Use
Example: The *Stingers* were defeated.	1	9	15. The *repetition* gets boring after a while.	15. ___	___
1. You *expect* me to believe that?	1. ___	___	16. Lunch was just *soup*.	16. ___	___
2. She is a tennis *star*.	2. ___	___	17. He drives *carefully*.	17. ___	___
3. *What!* It can't be true!	3. ___	___	18. He took her *advice*.	18. ___	___
4. *Green* creatures live there.	4. ___	___	19. Your cousin is *on* the run.	19. ___	___
5. Give *them* directions to Halifax.	5. ___	___	20. Up the trail came *Jim*.	20. ___	___
6. He seems *unfriendly*.	6. ___	___	21. We rented *a* car.	21. ___	___
7. No one came with *me*.	7. ___	___	22. She was poor *but* dishonest.	22. ___	___
8. Aren't *these* your keys?	8. ___	___	23. The path was *muddy*.	23. ___	___
9. Her son looks *like* her.	9. ___	___	24. She looks *good* in red.	24. ___	___
10. *Whom* did your friend see?	10. ___	___	25. I was *too* surprised to answer.	25. ___	___
11. The delegates elected McLaughlin *leader*.	11. ___	___	26. Repeat the first *step*.	26. ___	___
12. *Oh,* so that's it!	12. ___	___	27. *Who* is afraid of them?	27. ___	___
13. He does *well* in tests.	13. ___	___	28. Isn't *this* the street?	28. ___	___
14. She spoke *very* slowly.	14. ___	___	29. He played *very* well.	29. ___	___
			30. *Since* he was late for class, he ran.	30. ___	___

31. **Look** at the flags!   31. _____ _____

32. The mayor gave **Thompson** an order.   32. _____ _____

33. He ran **quickly.**   33. _____ _____

34. **"Hurrah!"** we yelled.   34. _____ _____

35. The stranger seemed unusually **hesitant.**   35. _____ _____

36. **Has** he **called** yet?   36. _____ _____

37. She is very **generous.**   37. _____ _____

38. **Biology** is her major.   38. _____ _____

39. **Hey,** that's my sandwich!   39. _____ _____

40. **Everyone** went to the party except me.   40. _____ _____

41. He seems **truly** sorry.   41. _____ _____

42. Yes, I **saw** her standing there.   42. _____ _____

43. It was a **silly** remark.   43. _____ _____

44. She asked **about** a job.   44. _____ _____

45. **Which** will be selected?   45. _____ _____

46. Will you tell him, **or** shall I?   46. _____ _____

47. The mayor declared the mall **open.**   47. _____ _____

48. His chances seem **good.**   48. _____ _____

49. Iron **and** zinc are metals.   49. _____ _____

50. The current was **swift.**   50. _____ _____

8. GRAMMAR: COMPLEMENTS

(Study G-3.2B.)

Write the number that tells how the boldface complement **is used:**

1. direct object   3. subjective complement
2. indirect object   4. objective complement

Example: Alex and Mallory took the **car.**   __1__

1. He has been an **environmentalist** for thirty years.   1. _____
2. This milk smells **sour.**   2. _____
3. Chelios gave **Kordic** a shove.   3. _____
4. He is writing his **memoirs.**   4. _____
5. They elected Sandra **head** of the committee.   5. _____
6. How can something taste **"light"**?   6. _____
7. Is he to be a **candidate**?   7. _____
8. Please give **me** your address.   8. _____
9. Alberta made Edmonton its **capital.**   9. _____
10. She lent me a **map** of Warsaw.   10. _____
11. Give **me** your solemn promise.   11. _____
12. She built her own hi-fi **set.**   12. _____
13. She sounds **happier** every day.   13. _____
14. He brings his **lunch** with him.   14. _____
15. The university offered **her** an opportunity to do research.   15. _____
16. He has my best **wishes.**   16. _____
17. She is a talented **actress.**   17. _____
18. Hamlet thought his mother **frail.**   18. _____
19. Pamela won a **scholarship.**   19. _____
20. Have you sent **copies** of the minutes to the members?   20. _____
21. **Whom** did you meet yesterday?   21. _____
22. Who designed the **plaque**?   22. _____
23. She is the **goaltender** now.   23. _____
24. Will you give **me** a chance?   24. _____
25. The sun on my back felt **good.**   25. _____
26. Politicians will promise **us** anything.   26. _____

27. She gave me no **chance** to object.   27. _____
28. She is writing an **editorial.**   28. _____
29. They have been studying **Greek** for a semester.   29. _____
30. She has been earning **money** ever since she was eleven years old.   30. _____
31. Either she or I will call **you.**   31. _____
32. I gave **him** my coin collection.   32. _____
33. His objection sounded **foolish.**   33. _____
34. **Which** did she choose?   34. _____
35. I named him my **beneficiary.**   35. _____
36. Were they the state **champions** last year?   36. _____
37. She is a **professor** at the local community college.   37. _____
38. She gave **me** no clue regarding her identity.   38. _____
39. That will be **all,** Hudson.   39. _____
40. I made an **appointment** with my new adviser.   40. _____
41. She became an **administrator.**   41. _____
42. I agreed to consider his **offer.**   42. _____
43. He considered her a **genius.**   43. _____
44. Choose your **weapons** carefully, gentlemen.   44. _____
45. The company made her **manager** of the branch office.   45. _____
46. Wasn't that **unfortunate** about Aunt Sally?   46. _____
47. Give **me** the key to your office.   47. _____
48. She likes **opera and ballet.**   48. _____
49. He tends to be **irresponsible** at times.   49. _____
50. He decided to give the rowboat a **coat** of red paint.   50. _____

9. GRAMMAR: COMPLEMENTS

(Study G-3.2B.)

Write the number that tells how the boldface complement **is used:**

1. direct object   **4. subjective complement (noun)**
2. objective complement (noun)   **5. subjective complement (pronoun)**
3. objective complement (adjective)   **6. subjective complement (adjective)**

Example: Hana is a *nurse.*   __4__

1. Anne received an anonymous *letter.*   1. _____
2. Jo was *dejected* after the loss.   2. _____
3. We considered Hal a *clown.*   3. _____
4. The music sounded *tuneless.*   4. _____
5. Wasn't that a great *dessert*?   5. _____
6. She named Roger her *assistant.*   6. _____
7. The judge declared him *insane.*   7. _____
8. Who threw out the first *pitch*?   8. _____
9. The dessert tasted *good.*   9. _____
10. Pat has been a *salesperson.*   10. _____
11. It was *he* who telephoned.   11. _____
12. Close the *door* quietly.   12. _____
13. The heat made us all *drowsy.*   13. _____
14. The experience was *unpleasant.*   14. _____
15. We met *them* backstage at the Elgin.   15. _____
16. The soup smelled very *good.*   16. _____
17. She is the construction *manager.*   17. _____
18. I consider her very *rude.*   18. _____
19. He recently bought a *ranch.*   19. _____
20. We elected her *treasurer.*   20. _____
21. This had been her *objective.*   21. _____
22. It is *we* who are responsible.   22. _____
23. Please leave the *key* with me.   23. _____
24. I denied that it was *I* who called.   24. _____
25. She studies *Russian* with a tutor.   25. _____
26. We consider her *honest.*   26. _____

27. *What* is the answer to the riddle?   27. _____
28. He has had great *recognition.*   28. _____
29. Klein had been *mayor* for many years.   29. _____
30. He did not seem particularly *worried.*   30. _____
31. She is *someone* you can trust.   31. _____
32. He enjoys *fishing* in the lake.   32. _____
33. She runs a *marathon* each year.   33. _____
34. June's hobby is *sculpture.*   34. _____
35. He must have been sound *asleep.*   35. _____
36. Alexandra has no *lack* of intelligence.   36. _____
37. Our interest in her career made her very *happy.*   37. _____
38. Was it *you* who wrote the essay?   38. _____
39. Did you find the *dictionary*?   39. _____
40. Are you the office *manager*?   40. _____
41. Is the victim *anyone* I know?   41. _____
42. Tyson defeated *everyone* who challenged him.   42. _____
43. The culprit was *neither* of the children originally suspected.   43. _____
44. His confidence was *shaken.*   44. _____
45. They made him a good *offer.*   45. _____
46. I appointed him *bailiff.*   46. _____
47. I appointed *him* bailiff.   47. _____
48. She usually felt *neglected.*   48. _____
49. She considers him *stupid.*   49. _____
50. Elliot convinced us *completely.*   50. _____

10. GRAMMAR: NOUN AND PRONOUN USE

(Study G-3 and G-6.)

Write the number that tells how each boldface noun or pronoun **is used**.
Use the first column for the first boldface word, the second column for the second.

1. subject   **4. subjective complement**   **7. appositive**
2. direct object   **5. objective complement**   **8. direct address**
3. indirect object   **6. object of preposition**

Example: The *Infantry* stormed the *barricades.*   <u> 1 </u> <u> 2 </u>

1. *Debris* from the *wreck* was strewn everywhere.   1. ____ ____

2. Some of his fellow *MPs* considered *Crosswell* somewhat unfair.   2. ____ ____

3. That must have been the *reason* that she told *us.*   3. ____ ____

4. His unorthodox behavior made *Singer* the *object* of criticism.   4. ____ ____

5. Canadian Press appointed *Huang* its chief Asian *correspondent.*   5. ____ ____

6. Dorothy, his *sister,* was with him when he revisited the *house.*   6. ____ ____

7. Down the library steps came *Anna,* her arms filled with reference *books.*   7. ____ ____

8. Having completed the test, she put her *paper* on the instructor's *desk* and left.   8. ____ ____

9. There are fourteen *students* whom the dean has named campus *assistants.*   9. ____ ____

10. Because she seemed genuinely interested, we told the *dean* our *troubles.*   10. ____ ____

11. *Toronto* will again be the **site** of the Grey Cup.   11. ____ ____

12. Having bought season *tickets,* I saw *most* of the Jays' games.   12. ____ ____

13. First read the *instructions;* then answer the *questions* carefully.   13. ____ ____

14. Although he knew the *answers* to most of the *questions,* he did not finish the test.   14. ____ ____

15. She gave each *student* an *opportunity* to try out for a part in the play.   15. ____ ____

16. It is, my fellow *students,* time for you to give *me* your close attention.   16. ____ ____

17. *He* thought about the *day* when he first met Cynthia.   17. ____ ____

18. The club *president* invited the members to suggest a *program* for the semester.   18. ____ ____

19. My Uncle Bruno has made *me vice-president* of his shoe factory.   19. ____ ____

20. General Grapeshot's unorthodox *tactics* bewildered the *enemy.*   20. ____ ____

21. Unless I am misinformed, she considers *herself* a *nonconformist.*   21. ____ ____

22. Dr. Ricardo promised *Gary* that the exam results would be *posted.*   22. ____ ____

23. There are, *ladies and gentlemen,* many *opportunities* to hear good speakers.   23. ____ ____

24. "Wasn't *he* invited?" asked *Hilda,* my roommate.   24. ____ ____

25. We asked the *speaker,* a former Olympic *medalist,* to speak on physical fitness.   25. ____ ____

18

11. GRAMMAR: NOUN, PRONOUN, AND ADJECTIVE USE

(Study G-3, G-5, and G-6.)

In the first column, write the number (**1** to **3**) of the **part of speech** of the boldface word.
In the second column, write the number (**4** to **9**) that tells how the word **is used:**

1. noun	4. subject	7. subjective complement
2. pronoun	5. direct object	8. objective complement
3. adjective	6. indirect object	9. object of preposition

	Part of Speech	Use		Part of Speech	Use
Example: Music filled the *air*.	_1_	_5_	17. Will *someone* please help me?	17. ___	___
1. I lent him some *money*.	1. ___	___	18. The jury found him *guilty*.	18. ___	___
2. *Jacques* made the first team.	2. ___	___	19. She tried to appear *poised*.	19. ___	___
3. I named *her* my successor.	3. ___	___	20. He has many *friends*.	20. ___	___
4. We elected him *secretary*.	4. ___	___	21. She sent *everyone* a thank-you note.	21. ___	___
5. Duncan has been a commercial *pilot* for ten years.	5. ___	___	22. Her story sounds *plausible*.	22. ___	___
6. The gift is for *her*.	6. ___	___	23. Is *this* your notebook?	23. ___	___
7. He has been *eager* to visit this country.	7. ___	___	24. Paolo removed the *books* from his locker.	24. ___	___
8. I gave *Sofia* a book.	8. ___	___	25. The results proved *interesting*.	25. ___	___
9. Boris became a *chemist*.	9. ___	___	26. *Neither* of us went.	26. ___	___
10. The puppy seemed *timid* when he first arrived.	10. ___	___	27. Give *her* A for effort.	27. ___	___
11. The report is of interest to *us*.	11. ___	___	28. He became an able *administrator*.	28. ___	___
12. Jogging keeps her *healthy*.	12. ___	___	29. Can you give *us* a hint?	29. ___	___
13. Give *us* a few good men.	13. ___	___	30. Few people today are afraid of *flying*.	30. ___	___
14. Is *he* your cousin?	14. ___	___			
15. She lives in *Winnipeg*.	15. ___	___			
16. Willy became *frightened* by all his failures.	16. ___	___			

12. GRAMMAR: VERB TENSE

(Study G-4.)

Write the number of the **tense** of the boldface verb:

1. present	**4.** present perfect (*have* or *has*)
2. past	**5.** past perfect (*had*)
3. future (*shall* or *will*)	**6.** future perfect (*shall have* or *will have*)

Example: You **spoke** too soon.   __2__

1. The sun **sets** in the west.   1. _____

2. He **will** surely **write** us soon.   2. _____

3. Next summer, we **shall have lived** in
   this house for ten years.   3. _____

4. The Allens **have planted** a vegetable
   garden.   4. _____

5. By noon he **will have finished** the
   whole job.   5. _____

6. Here **is** the six o'clock news.   6. _____

7. **Shall** we **reserve** a copy for you?   7. _____

8. The widow's savings **melted** away.   8. _____

9. I **had** not **expected** to see her.   9. _____

10. Carol **sends** her love.   10. _____

In the blank at the right, write the number of the **verb ending,** if any, that should appear at each bracketed space:

0. no ending   1. *s* or *es*   2. *ed* or *d*   3. *ing*

Example: The sun rise[ ] beyond that low hill.   __1__

The brown cliffs rise[1] directly from the gray sea; no buffer beach come[2] between them. The waves

have pound[3] the granite base of that cliff for ages but have fail[4] to wear[5] it away. Now, as always,

great white gulls circle[6] just above the foam, seeking fish that are destine[7] to become their dinner.

Years ago, when I first gather[8] the courage to approach[9] the cliff's sheer edge and peer[10] over, I

imagine[11] what it would be like if I tumble[12] over and plummet[13] into that seething surf.

I was an imaginative youth, and the thought fascinate[14] me then. At that time I was try[15] desperately

though unsuccessfully to win the heart of a dark-haired local girl, but she had been continually reject[16]

me, and her attitude had turn[17] my thoughts to suicide. I might, in fact, have hurl[18] myself over the

edge, except for one fact: My knees have always turn[19] to jelly at the mere thought of do[20] it.

Today, as a man of thirty, I can look[21] back on those years and laugh[22] . Yet even now, whenever

I approach[23] that treacherous edge, a chill run[24] through me. It is as if something inside me is say[25],

1. _____
2. _____
3. _____
4. _____
5. _____
6. _____
7. _____
8. _____
9. _____
10. _____
11. _____
12. _____
13. _____
14. _____

"Someday you will hurl[26] yourself over. You know[27] it." I have been haunt[28] by that thought ever since that girl reject[29] me, and I probably will always be obsess[30] by it—until the end.

15. _____
16. _____
17. _____
18. _____
19. _____
20. _____
21. _____
22. _____
23. _____
24. _____
25. _____
26. _____
27. _____
28. _____
29. _____
30. _____

13. GRAMMAR: VERBS—KIND, VOICE, AND MOOD

(Study G-4.)

Write **1** if the boldface verb is **transitive**.
Write **2** if it is **intransitive**.
Write **3** if it is a **linking** verb.

Example: The house *looks* fine. ___3___

1. Jenny *kissed* me when we met. 1. _____
2. Kitty *jogs* for two kilometers every morning. 2. _____
3. Your laughter *sounds* bitter. 3. _____
4. *Lay* your books on the table. 4. _____
5. The window *opened* onto the bay. 5. _____
6. Dr. Smiley *has* a fine reputation. 6. _____

7. The island *lay* fifty kilometers off the mainland. 7. _____
8. The last express *has* already *left.* 8. _____
9. Sue *lay* down for a short rest. 9. _____
10. The childhood playmates *remained* friends for life. 10. _____
11. The milk *smells* sour. 11. _____
12. The directions *seem* simple enough. 12. _____
13. The express *arrived* ten minutes late. 13. _____

Write **1** if the boldface verb is in the **active** voice.
Write **2** if it is in the **passive** voice.

Example: Lefty *threw* another strike. ___1___

1. Visitors *are* not *permitted* aboard the aircraft. 1. _____
2. One name *was* inadvertently *omitted* from the list. 2. _____
3. The conductor *cannot make* change for passengers. 3. _____
4. Man *proposes,* God disposes. 4. _____
5. The meeting *was called* to order. 5. _____
6. The ancient city *was* totally *destroyed* by a volcanic eruption. 6. _____
7. An unfortunate error *has been made.* 7. _____

8. Stan *has found* the letter. 8. _____
9. The witness *faltered* under the vigorous cross-examination. 9. _____
10. The robbery *could have occurred* about noon. 10. _____
11. The fishing treaty *will be signed* next month. 11. _____
12. The left-fielder *threw out* the runner. 12. _____
13. Jorge's credit card application *was approved.* 13. _____
14. *Batman will have been seen* by millions before the end of the summer. 14. _____
15. The virus *was* susceptible to heat. 15. _____

Write the number of the **mood** of the boldface verb:

1. indicative   2. imperative   3. subjunctive

Example: If she *were* smart, she'd finish school first. ___3___

1. The semester *had ended.* 1. _____
2. They *are* cousins. 2. _____
3. *Kiss* me, you fool! 3. _____
4. He *is building* a house. 4. _____

5. Would that I *were* wealthy! 5. _____
6. *Send* my check to the bank. 6. _____
7. If I *were* you, I'd not worry. 7. _____
8. *Stay* away from the cliff. 8. _____
9. Rosa *offered* us some tea. 9. _____

10. Please **thank** her for me.   10. _____   13. **Hurry!**   13. _____

11. I wish you **were** here.   11. _____   14. I **hurried** to get home.   14. _____

12. They **were** late as usual.   12. _____   15. If this **be** treason, make the most of it. 15. _____

14. GRAMMAR: VERBALS

(Study G-4 and G-7.2.)

Classify each boldface verbal:

1. infinitive   3. present participle
2. gerund   4. past participle

Example: *To be* or not to be; that is the question.   1

1. Do you like *to watch* football?   1. _____
2. *Watching* the game, she grew bored.   2. _____
3. His pastime is *watching* football.   3. _____
4. The Prime Minister's first job was *to restore* confidence.   4. _____
5. She enjoys *winning* at chess.   5. _____
6. This is a good plan *to follow.*   6. _____
7. Our *talking* distracted him.   7. _____
8. I submitted a *word-processed* essay.   8. _____
9. *Frightened,* the seal pups retreated.   9. _____
10. She dislikes *barking* dogs.   10. _____
11. He was eager *to begin.*   11. _____
12. By *hurrying,* he caught the bus.   12. _____

13. *Seeing* us, she smiled.   13. _____
14. She enjoys *driving* sports cars.   14. _____
15. She objects to our *watching* her.   15. _____
16. Not *knowing* a soul, she was lonely.   16. _____
17. He spent too much time *watching* television.   17. _____
18. *Frightened,* he became cautious.   18. _____
19. Her plan is *to leave* early.   19. _____
20. *Amazed,* she began to laugh.   20. _____
21. The *frightened* children cried.   21. _____
22. *Swimming* is good exercise.   22. _____
23. *Stopping* Gretzky's shot was impossible that day.   23. _____
24. Yours is not *to reason* why.   24. _____
25. *Reducing* carbon dioxide emissions remains a top priority.   25. _____

In the first column, **classify** each boldface verbal:

1. infinitive   2. gerund

In the second column, write the number that tells how that verbal **is used:**

3. subject   5. subjective complement
4. direct object   6. object of preposition

Example: *Sleeping* until noon is no way to greet the day.   2   3

1. General Grapeshot always enjoyed *holding* surprise inspections.   1. _____ _____
2. *To invent* a better mousetrap had been her childhood dream.   2. _____ _____
3. Larry likes *working* with young children in summer camps.   3. _____ _____
4. The ambassador's first task was *to arrange* a summit meeting.   4. _____ _____
5. The suspect apparently had no intention of *admitting* the crime.   5. _____ _____
6. Antonio worried about *borrowing* money.   6. _____ _____
7. We tried *to stop* him from making an unwise decision.   7. _____ _____
8. Her one wish has always been *to travel* extensively in Europe.   8. _____ _____
9. *Writing* a letter of application was no problem for her.   9. _____ _____

15. GRAMMAR: ADJECTIVES AND ADVERBS

(Study G-5.)

Write **1** if the boldface adjective or adverb is used **correctly**.
Write **0** if it is used **incorrectly**.

Example: The Argos are playing **good** this year. ___0___

1. That sun feels **good.** 1. _____
2. The team shouldn't feel **badly** about losing that game. 2. _____
3. She was the **most talented** member of the pair. 3. _____
4. He keeps in **good** condition always. 4. _____
5. Speak **softly** and carry a big stick. 5. _____
6. He was very **frank** in his evaluation of her work. 6. _____
7. He spoke very **frankly** to us. 7. _____
8. Of the two girls, she is the **prettiest.** 8. _____
9. My head aches **bad.** 9. _____
10. The child looked **hungry.** 10. _____
11. The child looked **hungrily** at the food on the table. 11. _____
12. I comb my hair **different** now. 12. _____
13. Fleagle talks too **smooth** to be trusted. 13. _____
14. Was Alex hurt **bad**? 14. _____
15. He limps **considerably.** 15. _____
16. He seemed **real** honest. 16. _____
17. I told **most** everyone the news. 17. _____
18. The milk tasted **sour.** 18. _____
19. Do you intend to go to the concert tonight? **Sure,** I do. 19. _____
20. Reading Mordechai Richler is a **real** pleasure. 20. _____
21. The tamer glanced **nervously** at the angry tigers. 21. _____
22. The crowd seemed **nervous** also. 22. _____
23. The campus will look **differently** when the new buildings are completed. 23. _____
24. This is the **clearest** of the two explanations. 24. _____

25. The book is in **good** condition. 25. _____
26. I did **poor** in French this term. 26. _____
27. She always looks **good** in green. 27. _____
28. Ericson felt **badly** about having to fire the veteran employee. 28. _____
29. Daryl's excuse was far **more poorer** than Keith's. 29. _____
30. The attic smelled **musty.** 30. _____
31. She speaks very **well.** 31. _____
32. It rained **steady** for the whole month of June. 32. _____
33. The roses smell **sweet.** 33. _____
34. He tries **hard** to please everyone. 34. _____
35. The man shouted **loudly** at her. 35. _____
36. John is **near** seven feet tall. 36. _____
37. He talked **considerable** about his future plans. 37. _____
38. She donated a **considerable** sum of money to the project. 38. _____
39. The **smartest** of the twins is spoiled. 39. _____
40. The **smartest** of the triplets is spoiled. 40. _____
41. The coach looked **uneasily** at his players. 41. _____
42. He felt **uneasy** about the score. 42. _____
43. Do try to drive more **careful.** 43. _____
44. It was Bob's **most unique** idea ever. 44. _____
45. I knotted the rope **loosely.** 45. _____
46. Alexis arrived **considerable** later than the others. 46. _____
47. The street looked **strangely** to us. 47. _____
48. The child sounded **unhappy.** 48. _____
49. The car has run **good** since it was last repaired. 49. _____

50. He was ill, but he is **well** now.   50. _____

51. This is the **cheapest** of the two cars.   51. _____

52. The music sounded **good** throughout the hall.   52. _____

53. Simon was **really** apologetic to Dave.   53. _____

54. Her dress looks **expensive.**   54. _____

55. Bob drives too **fast.**   55. _____

56. He seemed very **serious** about keeping his appointment.   56. _____

57. The stuffed cabbage smelled **good.**   57. _____

58. We felt **badly** about missing the farewell party.   58. _____

59. Barry looked on **sadly.**   59. _____

60. Barry was **sad** all morning.   60. _____

16. GRAMMAR: ADJECTIVES AND ADVERBS

(Study G-5.)

Write **1** if the boldface adjective is used **correctly.**
Write **0** if it is used **incorrectly;** then write the correction in the second column.

Example: He hit the ball **good.**	_0_	_well_
1. Ben was the **fastest** of the two sprinters.	1. ____	_____
2. The Canucks felt **badly** about their tenth loss.	2. ____	_____
3. We played **poor** for two periods.	3. ____	_____
4. The little ones look **real** sleepy to me, Mother.	4. ____	_____
5. They play their music much, much too **loudly.**	5. ____	_____
6. Of Lear's three daughters, Cordelia was the **younger.**	6. ____	_____
7. Hulk thought **deep** for a while and then fell over.	7. ____	_____
8. **Uneasily** is the head that wears the crown.	8. ____	_____
9. Her clothes are always **tasty.**	9. ____	_____
10. I am quite **well,** thank you.	10. ____	_____

17. GRAMMAR: PRONOUNS—KIND AND CASE

(Study G-6.)

Classify each boldface pronoun:

1. personal pronoun
2. interrogative pronoun
3. relative pronoun
4. demonstrative pronoun
5. indefinite pronoun
6. reciprocal pronoun
7. reflexive pronoun
8. intensive pronoun

Example: *Who* is Sylvia?   __2__

1. I made him an offer that *he* could not refuse.   1. _____

2. *No one* expected the snow to last so long.   2. _____

3. *This* is another fine mess you've gotten us into!   3. _____

4. He has only *himself* to blame for his predicament.   4. _____

5. *Which* of the local high schools has the best hockey team?   5. _____

6. She is the executive *who* makes the key decisions in this company. 6. _____

7. I *myself* have no desire to explore the rough terrain of mountainous regions. 7. _____

8. The twins resembled *each other* in appearance and disposition.   8. _____

9. *Several* of the games went into overtime.   9. _____

10. Has *anyone* ever suggested that he might just be lazy?   10. _____

11. The five brothers depended on *one another* for moral support. 11. _____

12. These are my biology notes; *those* must be yours.   12. _____

13. *Who* do you think will be the successful candidate in the student-body election? 13. _____

14. *Each* of the hostages had begged to go home.   14. _____

15. *Neither* of the parties engaged in collective bargaining would budge from its position. 15. _____

Write the number of the **correct** pronoun choice.

Example: Grandpa ordered lunch for Billy and (1)*I* (2)*me.*   __2__

1. Three of (1)*we* (2)*us* jury members voted for acquittal.   1. _____

2. If you were (1)*I* (2)*me,* would you be willing to change your plans completely? 2. _____

3. May we—John and (1)*I* (2)*me*—join you for lunch in the cafeteria? 3. _____

4. Between you and (1)*I* (2)*me,* I feel quite uneasy about the outcome of the expedition. 4. _____

5. Were you surprised that the trophies were awarded to Julia and (1)*he* (2)*him*? 5. _____

6. It must have been (1)*they* (2)*them* who called on us last evening. 6. _____

7. Why not give (1)*we* (2)*us* students an opportunity to help determine the matter? 7. _____

8. Nobody but (1)*she* (2)*her* can answer that question.   8. _____

9. He is much more talented in dramatics than (1)*she* (2)*her.*   9. _____

10. The premier supported (1)*whoever* (2)*whomever* supported the premier. 10. _____

18. GRAMMAR: PRONOUN CASE

(Study G-6.2.)

In the first column, write the number of the **correct** pronoun choice.
In the second column, write the number of the **reason** for your choice:

Choice	Reason for Choice
1. subject form (nominative case)	**3. subject of verb**
	4. subjective complement
2. object form (objective case)	**5. direct object**
	6. indirect object
	7. object of preposition
	8. subject of infinitive

	Word Choice	Reason for Choice
Example: Marie studied with Burt and (1)*I* (2)*me.*	2	7
1. Kim begged Betsy and (1)*I* (2)*me* to stay up late.	1. ____	____
2. Do you think it was (1)*she* (2)*her* who poisoned the cocoa?	2. ____	____
3. Were you and (1)*he* (2)*him* surprised by the result?	3. ____	____
4. Fourteen of (1)*we* (2)*us* students signed a petition to reverse the ruling.	4. ____	____
5. The assignment gave (1)*she* (2)*her* no further trouble after it was explained.	5. ____	____
6. She greeted, with great cordiality, the guests (1)*who* (2)*whom* I had brought.	6. ____	____
7. Shall we give (1)*they* (2)*them* an opportunity to enter the briar?	7. ____	____
8. I invited (1)*he* (2)*him* to select topics on which students might speak easily.	8. ____	____
9. Girls like (1)*she* (2)*her* are something special.	9. ____	____
10. I was very much surprised to see (1)*he* (2)*him* at the art exhibit.	10. ____	____
11. Are you and (1)*he* (2)*him* both working in the school cafeteria this year?	11. ____	____
12. We asked Joan and (1)*he* (2)*him* to supervise the playground activities.	12. ____	____
13. She asked, "(1)*Who* (2)*Whom* is willing to take charge of the ticket sale?"	13. ____	____
14. The top students in the class were Charles and (1)*she* (2)*her.*	14. ____	____
15. All of (1)*we* (2)*us* freshmen were asked to report for an orientation session.	15. ____	____
16. It was (1)*he* (2)*him* who made all the arrangements for the dance.	16. ____	____
17. Give the scholarship money to (1)*whoever* (2)*whomever* has the highest grades.	17. ____	____
18. My two friends and (1)*I* (2)*me* decided to go on a boat ride around the bay.	18. ____	____
19. This argument is just between Dick and (1)*I* (2)*me.*	19. ____	____
20. My father always gave (1)*I* (2)*me* money for my tuition.	20. ____	____
21. My sister scolded (1)*I* (2)*me* for not writing to her more frequently.	21. ____	____
22. I expect to go to the picnic with (1)*whoever* (2)*whomever* asks me.	22. ____	____

23. If you were (1)*I* (2)*me,* would you consider going on a summer cruise?   23. _____ _____

24. Please ask (1)*whoever* (2)*whomever* is at the door to wait.   24. _____ _____

25. (1)*Who* (2)*Whom* is the speaker to be at the noon assembly?   25. _____ _____

26. Everyone was excused from class except Louise, Mary, and (1)*I* (2)*me.*   26. _____ _____

27. The host asked (1)*he* (2)*him* to sing another chorus.   27. _____ _____

28. Florence is as capable as (1)*he* (2)*him* of typing the minutes of the meeting.   28. _____ _____

29. I knew of no one who had encountered more difficulties than (1)*she* (2)*her.*   29. _____ _____

30. Nobody but (1)*he* (2)*him* had been able to qualify for an overseas scholarship.   30. _____ _____

31. I hope to be the first to congratulate (1)*he* (2)*him* on his success.   31. _____ _____

32. The Frisbee gently drifted toward Bonnie and (1)*I* (2)*me.*   32. _____ _____

33. The teacher asked (1)*we* (2)*us* to speak extemporaneously on acid rain.   33. _____ _____

34. Her brother is ten years younger than (1)*she* (2)*her.*   34. _____ _____

35. Fifty of (1)*we* (2)*us* agreed to raise money for a memorial plaque.   35. _____ _____

36. The Kaplans offered (1)*she* (2)*her* a job for the summer.   36. _____ _____

37. Are you and (1)*she* (2)*her* planning to live in New Brunswick?   37. _____ _____

38. Nobody but (1)*he* (2)*him* knows the combination to the school safe.   38. _____ _____

39. I had decided to ask (1)*he* (2)*him* to officiate at the ceremony.   39. _____ _____

40. My friends had refused to go on the excursion without (1)*I* (2)*me.*   40. _____ _____

41. I am certain that he is as deserving of praise as (1)*she* (2)*her.*   41. _____ _____

42. If you were (1)*I* (2)*me,* which courses would you select as electives?   42. _____ _____

43. (1)*Who* (2)*Whom* do you think will be the next leader?   43. _____ _____

44. Assign the task to (1)*whoever* (2)*whomever* is willing to undertake it.   44. _____ _____

45. She is a person (1)*who* (2)*whom* is, without question, destined to achieve success.   45. _____ _____

46. He is the author about (1)*who* (2)*whom* we shall be writing a paper.   46. _____ _____

47. Was it (1)*he* (2)*him* who became an all-Canadian football player?   47. _____ _____

48. The only choice left was between (1)*she* (2)*her* and him.   48. _____ _____

49. No one was critical of the performance but (1)*she* (2)*her.*   49. _____ _____

50. The instructor asked (1)*I* (2)*me* to appear on a panel with three of my classmates.   50. _____ _____

51. "Were you calling (1)*I* (2)*me?*" Jill asked as she entered the room.   51. _____ _____

52. Shouldn't we give (1)*she* (2)*her* an opportunity to state her opinion?   52. _____ _____

53. Marilyn and (1)*I* (2)*me* played the leads in *Romeo and Juliet* last year.   53. _____ _____

54. Both of (1)*we* (2)*us* agreed that the unaccustomed exercise had been too much for us.   54. _____ _____

55. Mr. Parker is probably a more competent editor than (1)*he* (2)*him* is a swimmer.   55. _____ _____

56. Imagine finally meeting (1)*he* (2)*him* after so many years of correspondence!   56. _____ _____

57. My mother asked one of the other tourists to photograph the twins and (1)*she* (2)*her* at the top of the CN Tower.   57. _____ _____

58. Do you suppose that (1)*he* (2)*him* will ever find time to come?   58. _____ _____

59. Everyone at the lake except (1)*I* (2)*me* is an ardent fisher.   59. _____ _____

60. Everyone but (1)*she* (2)*her* was there on time.   60. _____ _____

61. It was known that the officials wanted Gina rather than (1)*she* (2)*her.*   61. _____ _____

62. The student (1)*who* (2)*whom* Dr. Potter asked to answer wasn't prepared.   62. _____ _____

63. It was Holmes who noticed the footprints on the ceiling, not (1)*I* (2)*me.*   63. _____ _____

64. Watching the Flames win the Stanley Cup made our friends and (1)*we* (2)*us* very happy.   64. _____ _____

65. A dispute arose about (1)*who* (2)*whom* would pay the check.   65. _____ _____

66. She is the one (1)*who* (2)*whom* I am certain will win the award.   66. _____ _____

67. The scholarship will be given to (1)*whoever* (2)*whomever* deserves it most.   67. _____ _____

19. GRAMMAR: PRONOUN REFERENCE

(Study G-6.3.)

Write **1** if the boldface word is used **correctly.**
Write **0** if it is used **incorrectly.**

Example: Gulliver agreed with his master that *he* was a Yahoo.   __0__

1. David won the lottery and quit his job. *This* was unexpected.   1. _____
2. Betsy told Alison that *she* didn't follow through enough.   2. _____
3. Alf decided to drop out of St. Mary's. He later regretted *that* decision.   3. _____
4. On the white card, list the classes *that* you plan to take this year.   4. _____
5. Tom thought of Nick because *he* owed him a favor.   5. _____
6. In England, *they* call a truck a *lorry.*   6. _____
7. I was late filing my report, *which* greatly embarrassed me.   7. _____
8. On her return from Europe, *they* stopped her at Customs.   8. _____
9. She was able to complete college after earning a research assistantship. We greatly admired her for
   that.   9. _____
10. We suggested that the players stage *Falstaff,* but *it* was not well received.   10. _____
11. Reluctantly, the princess used her third wish, *which* canceled the first two thoughtless ones. 11. _____
12. They planned to climb sheer Mount Maguffey, a feat *that* no one had ever accomplished.   12. _____
13. Pat always wanted to be a television newscaster; thus she majored in *it* in college.   13. _____
14. Barkum denounced the use of arbitration in the dispute, *which* was not popular with the workers. 14. _____
15. *It* was well past midnight when the phone rang.   15. _____
16. The speaker kept scratching his head, a mannerism *that* proved distracting.   16. _____
17. *It* says in the paper that the Prime Minister's popularity is declining.   17. _____
18. When Pete retires, *they* will probably give him a gold watch.   18. _____
19. When Schultz presented his highly negative criticism of the play, the professor said she thought *it* was
    well written.   19. _____
20. Eric started taking pictures in high school. *This* interest led to a brilliant career in photography. 20. _____
21. *It* will probably not start snowing until Ken reaches home.   21. _____
22–23. In some vacation spots, *they* add the tip to your bill and then give poor service. *This* isn't
       a way to treat a customer.   22. _____
                                                                                                   23. _____
24–25. In some parts of wartime Europe *it* was so bad that *they* died like flies.   24. _____
                                                                                                   25. _____

20. GRAMMAR: PHRASES

(Study G-7.)

In the first column, write the number of the **one** set of underlined words that is a **prepositional phrase**.
In the second column, write the number that tells how that phrase is **used** in that sentence:

7. as adjective   8. as adverb

	Phrase	Use
Example: The starting pitcher for the Jays is a left-hander. 1 2 3	2	7
1. When we came downstairs, a cab was awaiting us at the curb. 1 2 3	1. ____	____
2. The red-brick building erected in the last century collapsed last week without warning. 1 2 3 4	2. ____	____
3. After each session the noted professor and his assistant answered the audience's 1 2 3 4 questions.	3. ____	____
4. What they saw before the door closed shocked them beyond belief. 1 2 3 4	4. ____	____
5. No one here has ever seen such consummate grace of style. 1 2 3 4	5. ____	____
6. The poetry of Wordsworth's early years is what his reputation rests on. 1 2 3	6. ____	____
7. This may be what you want, but it's not within my price range. 1 2 3 4	7. ____	____
8. A strange call like a crow's can worry us, for it means that enemy scouts are nearby. 1 2 3 4 5 6	8. ____	____
9. Since they knew who he was, they held him in spite of the law that forbids any such 1 2 3 4 5 detention. 6	9. ____	____
10. Through extended negotiations the disputing parties reached an agreement that had 1 2 3 long seemed impossible. 4	10. ____	____

If the words in boldface are **a verbal phrase** (infinitive, gerund, or participial), write **1** in the first column and **one** of the following numbers in the second column:

2. verbal phrase used as **adjective**
3. verbal phrase used as **adverb**
4. verbal phrase used as **noun**

If the boldface words are **not a verbal phrase**, write **0** in the first column and nothing in the second column.

	Phrase	Use
Example: *Singing in the rain* is a sure way to get wet.	1	4
Example: Gene is *singing in the rain* despite his cold.	0	
1. *Taking portrait photographs of children* is her means of earning a living.	1. ____	____

2. These days she is *taking portrait photographs of children* as her means of earning a living.

2. _____ _____

3. *To work in the theater,* she had to accept a low salary.

3. _____ _____

4. She devoted all her energies *to her work in the theater.*

4. _____ _____

5. Houses *constructed of stone* can last centuries.

5. _____ _____

6. The houses were *constructed of stone* to last centuries.

6. _____ _____

7. His idea of a thrill is *driving in stock-car races.*

7. _____ _____

8. *Driving in stock-car races,* he not only gets his thrills but earns prize money.

8. _____ _____

9. Nowadays he is *driving in stock-car races* for thrills and money.

9. _____ _____

10. He would like *to spend his life as a race driver.*

10. _____ _____

21. GRAMMAR: VERBAL PHRASES

(Study G-7.2.)

Classify each boldface verbal phrase:

1. **infinitive phrase** used as noun
2. **infinitive phrase** used as adjective
3. **infinitive phrase** used as adverb
4. **present participial phrase**
5. **past participial phrase**
6. **gerund phrase**

(Use the first column for the first phrase, the second column for the second.)

		5	6
Example: *Thrilled by her results,* Elaine began *applying to several colleges.*			
1. *Seeing the traffic worsen,* Adam chose *to wait until after rush hour.*	1.		
2. *Obtaining a ticket at that late hour* was not easy *to do.*	2.		
3. *Controlling acid rain* is a crucial step in *protecting our lakes and rivers.*	3.		
4. *Intrigued by what he was saying,* she forgot *to go to her science class.*	4.		
5. *Knowing his potential,* I agreed that John was the man *to select for the position.*	5.		
6. Try *to slip away* without *telling your friends where you are going.*	6.		
7. I can't help *admiring her;* did you object to *my praising her work*?	7.		
8. I appreciate *your helping us;* will you be able *to help us again*?	8.		
9. *Loaded down with library books,* she tried *to open the front door.*	9.		
10. *Preparing his history assignment* was not as hard *to do* as he had anticipated.	10.		
11. *Wearing caps and gowns,* the graduates began *to march into the auditorium.*	11.		
12. Sam tried *to run the whole race,* but he was too tired *to do more than a single lap.*	12.		
13. The speaker, *obviously resenting our interruptions,* frowned at us as we tried *to ask other questions.*	13.		
14. *Hiking seven kilometers over mountain trails* is sport *demanding endurance.*	14.		
15. The students left, *commenting enthusiastically about the speaker* and *hoping to have her return.*	15.		
16. To try to pass the test without *studying for it* was not a wise thing *to do.*	16.		
17. *Alarmed by the rapid spread of the measles epidemic,* the health authorities had no alternative but *to vaccinate as many children as possible.*	17.		
18. *Not having a college major in mind,* he began *to ask about required courses.*	18.		
19. *Not knowing her way in the strange city,* she stopped *to ask directions.*	19.		
20. She tried *to obtain the information* without *asking any direct questions.*	20.		
21. The student *waiting in your office* has two questions *to ask.*	21.		
22. *Careless camping* has been the cause of too many forests being *reduced to ashes.*	22.		

23. By *looking carefully,* he found an article that was easy *to understand.* 23. _____ _____

24. *Obviously surprised,* she had not known of our plan *to take her with us.* 24. _____ _____

25. Upon *hearing from my parents,* I decided *to go home for the weekend.* 25. _____ _____

22. GRAMMAR: PHRASES—REVIEW

(Study G-7.)

In the first column, **classify** each boldface phrase:

1. **prepositional phrase** 4. **gerund phrase**
2. **infinitive phrase**   5. **absolute phrase**
3. **participial phrase**

In the second column, tell how that phrase **is used:**

6. **as adjective**   7. **as adverb**   8. **as noun**

(For an absolute phrase, write nothing in the second column.)

		Phrase	Use
Example: The orders came *from on high.*		1	7
1. The woman standing **between the delegates** is an interpreter.	1.	____	____
2. The woman *standing between the delegates* is an interpreter.	2.	____	____
3. Tara looked for her zither everywhere **around the house.**	3.	____	____
4. *His insisting that he was right* made him unpopular with his associates.	4.	____	____
5. The committee voted **to adjourn immediately.**	5.	____	____
6. *Because of the storm,* the excursion around the lake had to be postponed.	6.	____	____
7. *To be the president of the group* pleased her very much.	7.	____	____
8. *During July and August,* many people go on vacation trips.	8.	____	____
9. *Flying a jet at supersonic speeds* has been Sally's dream since childhood.	9.	____	____
10. The agent *wearing an official badge* is the one to see about tickets.	10.	____	____
11. *The day being sunny and warm,* Sam decided to skip his English class.	11.	____	____
12. *Reminded of the grade on his last essay,* Sam ran all the way to class.	12.	____	____
13. *To help students make out programs,* counselors will be on duty all day.	13.	____	____
14. Garth was successful in *producing a long succession of hit shows.*	14.	____	____
15. The students left for many parts of the state, *the college year having ended.*	15.	____	____
16. The distinguished-looking man *in the blue suit* is the head of the company.	16.	____	____
17. *By working hard,* she was able to make up for lost time.	17.	____	____
18. By *working hard,* she was able to make up for lost time.	18.	____	____
19. Their ears were attuned *to any unusual sound.*	19.	____	____
20. I would appreciate *your letting us know your time of arrival.*	20.	____	____
21. Two crates *of oranges* were delivered to the restaurant.	21.	____	____
22. *Anticipating an overflow audience,* the custodian put extra chairs in the auditorium.	22.	____	____
23. A car *filled with students* left early this morning to arrange for the class picnic.	23.	____	____

24. I cannot help *thinking that he might have done better in the test.* 24. _____ _____

25. We were obliged to abandon our plans, *the boat having been damaged in a recent storm.* 25. _____ _____

26. We knew, *conditions being what they were,* that further progress was impossible. 26. _____ _____

27. *Doing my homework* interfered with my watching my favorite television program. 27. _____ _____

28. *Waving his arms and shouting,* John threatened everyone in the courtroom. 28. _____ _____

29. *Shouting and laughing,* the children splashed merrily in the swimming pool. 29. _____ _____

30. *Her experiment having been completed,* she left the science building and went home. 30. _____ _____

31. Maria's cat chewed the disk *with her economics essay* on it. 31. _____ _____

32. *Frightened by Maria's shrieks,* the cat hid in the laundry basket and ate socks for an hour. 32. _____ _____

33. *Professor Hacksaw having specifically warned all cat fanciers in the class,* Maria knew she had a problem. 33. _____ _____

34. *Backing up all files* was something she seldom did. 34. _____ _____

35. *Suddenly remembering that this time she had backed up the disk,* Maria decided to forgive Tigger. 35. _____ _____

36. *To convince Tigger that she wasn't angry,* she put out some tuna on a floppy disk. 36. _____ _____

37. *The time getting close to her physics lab,* Maria had to leave before Tigger emerged. 37. _____ _____

38. Once Maria had left, the cat leapt on her desk and sat *beside her computer* for a while. 38. _____ _____

39. *Having enjoyed the game of cat and disk,* Tigger looked on her desk for her history files. 39. _____ _____

40. This proves that *owning a cat* is only for those who make backups. 40. _____ _____

23. GRAMMAR: CLAUSES

(Study G-8.)

Classify each boldface clause:

1. **independent (main) clause**   2. **adjective clause**
                                      3. **adverb clause**   } **dependent (subordinate) clause**
                                      4. **noun clause**

Example: Do the dishes *when you're finished eating.*   __3__

1. Elizabethan theater companies performed *where they were welcome.*   1. _____
2. Elizabethan theater companies performed in towns *where they were welcome.*   2. _____
3. Elizabethan theater companies knew *where they were welcome.*   3. _____
4. The student *who made the top grade in the history quiz* is my roommate.   4. _____
5. *Whether I would be able to go to college* depended on whether I could find employment.   5. _____
6. *After Jud had written a paper for his English class,* he watched television.   6. _____
7. While I waited for a bus, *I chatted with friends.*   7. _____
8. The college counseling center offers help to anyone *who needs it.*   8. _____
9. There is much excitement *whenever election results are announced.*   9. _____
10. You may use my pen, but *please don't forget to return it to me afterwards.*   10. _____
11. My adviser suggested *that I enroll in a special science course.*   11. _____
12. My first impression was *that someone had been in my room quite recently.*   12. _____
13. The actress who had lost the Juno award *declared through clenched teeth that she was delighted just to have been nominated.*   13. _____
14. He dropped a letter in the mailbox; *then he went into the library.*   14. _____
15. Her reason for moving into the residence is *that she wishes to find new friends.*   15. _____
16. Why don't you sit here *until the rest of the class arrives*?   16. _____
17. The real estate mogul, *who is not known for his modesty,* has named yet another parking lot after himself.   17. _____
18. *Although he is fifty-two years old,* he is very youthful in appearance.   18. _____
19. I vividly recall the day *when I won the high school speech tournament.*   19. _____
20. She lived on a ranch *when she was in Alberta.*   20. _____
21. *Why don't you wait* until you have all the facts?   21. _____
22. She is a person *whom everyone respects and admires.*   22. _____
23. He thought carefully *in order that he might avoid further errors.*   23. _____
24. I said nothing except *that I had been unavoidably detained.*   24. _____
25. The hotel *where the Winter Carnival dance will be held* has not yet been selected.   25. _____
26. The trophy will be awarded to *whoever wins the contest.*   26. _____

27. The detective walked up the stairs; *he opened the door of the guest room.*   27. _____

28. Is this the book *that you asked us to order for you*?   28. _____

29. Smiling foolishly, Ramsey admitted *that there was no basis to the story.*   29. _____

30. Will you tell me *what your plans are for the summer months*?   30. _____

24. GRAMMAR: CLAUSES

(Study G-8.)

Identify the **dependent** clause in each sentence by writing its first and last words in the first two columns; in the third column, classify it as:

1. noun
2. adjective
3. adverb

	First	Last	Type
Example: The band was dividing the money when the police arrived.	when	arrived	3

1. The children played where there were lots of toys. 1. _____ _____ ___
2. The children looked for a room where there were lots of toys. 2. _____ _____ ___
3. The children knew where there were lots of toys. 3. _____ _____ ___
4. The student who complained about the food was given another helping. 4. _____ _____ ___
5. Whether Camille dyes his hair remains a mystery. 5. _____ _____ ___
6. After Jonathan had read the morning paper, he threw up his hands in despair. 6. _____ _____ ___
7. While I waited for Derwin, I was able to finish my crossword puzzle. 7. _____ _____ ___
8. Professor George gave extra help to anyone who asked for it. 8. _____ _____ ___
9. There is always a lot of anxiety whenever exams are held. 9. _____ _____ ___
10. The coach decided that I was not going to play that year. 10. _____ _____ ___
11. Once more, I waited until I had only one night to write my essay. 11. _____ _____ ___
12. Dr. Jackson, who prided himself on his fairness, declared Burton the winner. 12. _____ _____ ___
13. Although there was no chance of his accepting, I asked David for a date. 13. _____ _____ ___
14. I'll never forget Legree's face when I told him to leave. 14. _____ _____ ___
15. Hudson remarked that he too had trouble with calculus. 15. _____ _____ ___
16. It was the only mistake that I had ever seen Henning make. 16. _____ _____ ___
17. Nathan explained how his concern about its electrical system kept him from buying the car. 17. _____ _____ ___
18. Most of the audience had tears in their eyes when Juliet died. 18. _____ _____ ___
19. I told Pat that I would love to meet his sister. 19. _____ _____ ___
20. Jill had to leave her office, which was being repainted. 20. _____ _____ ___

25. GRAMMAR: NOUN AND ADJECTIVE CLAUSES

(Study G-8.2.)

Classify each boldface dependent clause:

	Noun Clause	*Adjective Clause*

1. used as **subject**   **3.** used as **subjective complement**   **5.** nonrestrictive (nonessential)
2. used as **direct object**   **4.** used as **object of preposition**   **6.** restrictive (essential)

Example: *That she was incompetent* was clear.   _____1_____

1. *Who was the better skier* remained unresolved.   1. _____

2. The programmer *who wrote the new computer game* retired at twenty.   2. _____

3. I don't see how anyone could object to *what the speaker said.*   3. _____

4. Leo married Elsa Vidgren, a young woman *whom he had met in high school.*   4. _____

5. *What he wanted us to do for him* seemed utterly impossible.   5. _____

6. Give the four books to *whoever is going to the library.*   6. _____

7. This is a problem *that almost everyone encounters sooner or later.*   7. _____

8. My worst fear is *that I'll be trapped in an elevator and have to listen to the music.*   8. _____

9. Grindley is a person *who seems to thrive on hard work.*   9. _____

10. We visited the area *where gold had first been discovered.*   10. _____

11. Alexander Graham Bell, *who is famous for his invention of the telephone,* also experimented with
heavier-than-air aircraft.   11. _____

12. She little realized on setting out *that the journey would take ten years.*   12. _____

13. The long black limousine, *which had been waiting in front of the building,* sped away suddenly.   13. _____

14. *Whether or not we shall travel by plane* will be determined by the group.   14. _____

15. *What you decide to do now* is critically important.   15. _____

16. The woman *who wrote this letter* shows remarkable perspicacity.   16. _____

17. The jackpot will be won by *whoever holds the lucky number.*   17. _____

18. Naphtha, *which is highly flammable,* is no longer much used for cleaning.   18. _____

19. Plato argued *that artists should be censored.*   19. _____

20. The alarm sounded at a moment *when the students were seated in the gymnasium.*   20. _____

21. We were appalled by *what he had to tell us regarding the episode.*   21. _____

22. *That the war was already lost* could no longer be denied.   22. _____

23. We visited the courthouse *where the Donald Marshall trial had been held.*   23. _____

24. Len enrolled in astronomy, a subject *that had always appealed to him.*   24. _____

25. The truth is *that she had studied the wrong chapter.*   25. _____

26. GRAMMAR: ADVERB CLAUSES

(Study G-8.2B.)

Classify each boldface adverb clause:

1. time (*when, after, until, etc.*)   6. condition (*if, unless, etc.*)
2. place (*where, wherever*)   7. concession (*although, though*)
3. manner (*as, as if, as though*)   8. result (*that*)
4. cause (*because, since*)   9. degree or comparison (*as, than*)
5. purpose (*that, so that, etc.*)

Example: There would be a recount *if I had my way.*   ___6___

1. *Because I could not stop for Death,* he kindly stopped for me.   1. _____

2. The candidate was willing to speak *wherever she could find an audience.*   2. _____

3. Ben ran *as if his life depended on it.*   3. _____

4. She has always been able to read much faster *than her brother has.*   4. _____

5. *If I were you,* I would not ask for special consideration at this time.   5. _____

6. He planned the program *so that he might have time for an occasional bridge game.*   6. _____

7. Half of the audience left *before the concert was half over.*   7. _____

8. People are said to be only as old *as they think they are.*   8. _____

9. He read extensively *in order that he might be well prepared for the test.*   9. _____

10. *Unless the weather changes,* I won't wear my parka.   10. _____

11. *Although his grades were satisfactory,* he did not qualify for the scholarship.   11. _____

12. She had worried so much *that she could no longer function effectively.*   12. _____

13. *Whether or not you are selected,* you will be notified.   13. _____

14. *Since you say that you will be happier elsewhere,* I will not oppose your leaving.   14. _____

15. She was so excited *that she had trouble going to sleep that night.*   15. _____

16. Do not complete the rest of the form *until you have seen your adviser.*   16. _____

17. *Although he was only 5 feet 5 inches tall,* he was determined to be a basketball star.   17. _____

18. *Because Einstein had been a poor student,* his parents did not predict a successful career for him. 18. _____

19. Roberts preferred to go *where no one would recognize him.*   19. _____

20. *If the litmus paper turns red,* the substance is an acid.   20. _____

21. Andres hit the ball so far *that it cleared the center-field fence.*   21. _____

22. She usually received better grades *than her brother did.*   22. _____

23. This is as far *as the elevator goes.*   23. _____

24. He keeps silent *unless he is certain of his facts,* doesn't he?   24. _____

25. She smiled *as if she knew something not known to the rest of us.*   25. _____

27. GRAMMAR: KINDS OF SENTENCES

(Study G-8.3.)

Classify each sentence:

1. simple   2. compound   3. complex   4. compound-complex

(Any subordinate clauses in the first ten sentences are in boldface.)

Example: He opened the throttle, and the boat sped off.   __2__

1. Mr. Toad still insisted *that he was an excellent driver.*   1. _____

2. The king, *who was scornful of his advisers,* declared war; he soon regretted his rashness. 2. _____

3. Completion of campus buildings will be delayed *unless funds become available.*   3. _____

4. Consider the matter carefully *before you decide;* your decision will be final.   4. _____

5. This year, either Hull or Orr will be inducted into the Hockey Hall of Fame.   5. _____

6. Geoffrey Chaucer, *who wrote* **The Canterbury Tales,** died in 1400.   6. _____

7. The storm, *which had caused much damage,* subsided; we continued on our hike.   7. _____

8. We waited *until all the spectators had left the gymnasium.*   8. _____

9. The site for the theater having been selected, construction was begun.   9. _____

10. The skies darkened; the rains came.   10. _____

11. His career as a spy having ended, he settled in Québec and began his memoirs.   11. _____

12. The beaches are beautiful and uncrowded, and the sun shines most of the time.   12. _____

13. His chief worry was that he might reveal the secret by talking in his sleep.   13. _____

14. Cyrano was sensitive about his long nose; he always imagined that people were making jokes about it.   14. _____

15. The story that appeared in the school paper contained a few inaccuracies.   15. _____

16. The police officer picked up the package and inspected it carefully.   16. _____

17. Because she was eager to get an early start, Sue packed the night before.   17. _____

18. Give the book on ceramics to whoever wants it; we no longer need it.   18. _____

19. Noticing the late arrivals, the speaker motioned them to be seated.   19. _____

20. Who had killed his father was not in doubt; if Hamlet would take his revenge was.   20. _____

21. The suspect went to the police station and turned himself in.   21. _____

22. She is a person who is meticulous about detail.   22. _____

23. Her father, who is an amateur photographer, won a prize in a recent contest.   23. _____

24. Summer, fall, spring—I love any season but winter.   24. _____

25. The house that we wanted had been sold; therefore, we had to look for another one.   25. _____

26. Scientists from all over the world convened to discuss the increasingly serious problem of the greenhouse effect.   26. _____

27. Several blockbuster movies were released during the summer, and all were sequels to earlier box-office successes.   27. _____

28. The Chinese government arrested hundreds of persons whom they suspected of pro-democracy sympathies.   28. _____

29. The library contained several boxes of Margaret Mead's field notes which had been made when she worked with the people of New Guinea.   29. _____

30. Although Amy's choreography won praise from the critics, she wasn't satisfied, and she and her company spent the next morning reworking it.   30. _____

31. Did she appear tired?   31. _____

32. The Royal Commission held hearings all through the summer but refused to say when it would release its final report.   32. _____

33. Demand for tickets was so strong for the Sniveling Fools concert that the promoters scheduled a second.   33. _____

34. Joyce, who was watching her weight, turned down the double-fudge chewy brownie and instead ordered a bowl of alfalfa bran.   34. _____

35. The Canucks were surprise winners, having defeated the Oilers in six games. 35. _____

28. GRAMMAR: AGREEMENT—SUBJECT AND VERB

(Study G-9.1.)

Write the number of the **correct** choice.

Example: One of my favorite programs (1)*was* (2)*were* canceled.   ___1___

 1. Neither the researcher nor the subject (1)*has* (2)*have* any idea which is the placebo.   1. _____

 2. Economics (1)*is* (2)*are* what the students are most interested in.   2. _____

 3. Babysitting my cousin's three children (1)*has* (2)*have* exhausted me.   3. _____

 4. Not one of the nominees (1)*has* (2)*have* won a Juno before.   4. _____

 5. (1)*Does* (2)*Do* each of the questions count the same number of points?   5. _____

 6. The number of college students (1)*has* (2)*have* decreased in recent years.   6. _____

 7. *Ninety-nine* (1)*is* (2)*are* hyphenated because it is a compound number.   7. _____

 8. The Queen, surrounded by a dozen security agents, (1)*was* (2)*were* to arrive by noon.   8. _____

 9. Both the secretary and the treasurer (1)*was* (2)*were* asked to submit reports.   9. _____

10. Everyone in the auditorium (1)*was* (2)*were* startled by the announcement.   10. _____

11. *Women* (1)*is* (2)*are* a common noun, plural in number.   11. _____

12. Every male and female athlete (1)*was* (2)*were* greeted by the Prince.   12. _____

13. There (1)*is* (2)*are* a briefcase, a typewriter, and a tape recorder in the office.   13. _____

14. Ten dollars (1)*is* (2)*are* too much to pay for that book.   14. _____

15. (1)*Is* (2)*Are* there any doughnuts left?   15. _____

16. Neither Margaret nor I (1)*is* (2)*am* (3)*are* going to the fair.   16. _____

17. Each of the suitors (1)*was* (2)*were* sure the princess preferred him.   17. _____

18. (1)*Is* (2)*Are* your father and brother coming to see you graduate tomorrow?   18. _____

19. A typewriter and a sheet of paper (1)*was* (2)*were* all that he needed at the moment.   19. _____

20. There (1)*is* (2)*are* just one chocolate and two vanilla cookies left in my lunch box.   20. _____

21. (1)*Does* (2)*Do* Coach Jasek and the players know about the special award?   21. _____

22. My three weeks' vacation (1)*was* (2)*were* more enjoyable than I had anticipated.   22. _____

23. The only thing that annoyed the speaker (1)*was* (2)*were* the frequent interruptions.   23. _____

24. (1)*Hasn't* (2)*Haven't* either of the officers submitted a written statement?   24. _____

25. The news of his spectacular achievements (1)*comes* (2)*come* as a surprise to all of us.   25. _____

26. On the table (1)*was* (2)*were* a pen, a pad of paper, and two rulers.   26. _____

27. It's remarkable that the entire class (1)*is* (2)*are* passing this semester.   27. _____

28. It (1)*was* (2)*were* your uncle and your cousin who came to see you.   28. _____

29. There (1)*is* (2)*are* many opportunities for part-time employment on campus.   29. _____

30. (1)*Is* (2)*Are* algebra and chemistry required courses?   30. _____

31. One of his three instructors (1)**has** (2)**have** offered to write a letter of recommendation.

31. _____

32. (1)**Does** (2)**Do** either of your brothers-in-law have jobs?

32. _____

33. Neither I nor my sister (1)**expects** (2)**expect** to graduate in June.

33. _____

29. GRAMMAR: AGREEMENT—SUBJECT AND VERB

(Study G-9.1.)

Write the number of the **correct** choice.

Example: Neither Sarah nor her parents (1)*was* (2)*were* ready to leave the fairgrounds.　　　　　　　　　　_2_

1. Virtually every painting and every sculpture Picasso did (1)*is* (2)*are* worth over a million dollars.　　1. _____

2. There on the table (1)*was* (2)*were* my wallet and my key chain.　　2. _____

3. Neither the documentary about beekeeping nor the two shows about Iceland (1)*was* (2)*were* successful in the ratings.　　3. _____

4. Each of the players (1)*hopes* (2)*hope* to make the first team.　　4. _____

5. German measles (1)*is* (2)*are* a disease of short duration.　　5. _____

6. Sitting on the stairway (1)*was* (2)*were* the instructor and four of her students.　　6. _____

7. *Voyages to the Stars* (1)*is* (2)*are* truly exciting reading.　　7. _____

8. A political convention, with its candidates, delegates, and reporters, (1)*seems* (2)*seem* like bedlam.　　8. _____

9. In the auditorium (1)*was* (2)*were* gathered many students to honor the new officers.　　9. _____

10. Each of the visitors (1)*has* (2)*have* been assigned a parking space.　　10. _____

11. (1)*Was* (2)*Were* either Rabbi Levine or Father O'Connor asked to speak at the assembly?　　11. _____

12. My scissors (1)*was* (2)*were* not where I had left them yesterday.　　12. _____

13. His courage, as well as his ability, (1)*makes* (2)*make* him much admired by many.　　13. _____

14. High-powered cars (1)*has* (2)*have* become his main interest in life.　　14. _____

15. His baseball and his glove (1)*was* (2)*were* all Nick was permitted to take to the game.　　15. _____

16. Neither my friends nor I (1)*expects* (2)*expect* to go on the overnight trip.　　16. _____

17. My coach and mentor (1)*is* (2)*are* Mr. Graham.　　17. _____

18. Among her most valued possessions (1)*was* (2)*were* a locket and a bracelet.　　18. _____

19. The committee (1)*is* (2)*are* unable to come to a decision regarding the scholarship.　　19. _____

20. Your carriage, along with its driver and two footmen, (1)*awaits* (2)*await* your every command.　　20. _____

21. Where (1)*is* (2)*are* the canoe and the sailboat?　　21. _____

22. Corinne, as well as her two cousins, (1)*intends* (2)*intend* to spend the summer here.　　22. _____

23. (1)*Has* (2)*Have* either of the books on architecture been returned to the library?　　23. _____

24. Neither criticism nor frequent failures (1)*was* (2)*were* enough to retard his progress.　　24. _____

25. Where (1)*is* (2)*are* your raincoat and boots?　　25. _____

26. The warden, as well as three of the guards, (1)*has* (2)*have* been indicted.　　26. _____

27. She is the only one of six candidates who (1)*refuses* (2)*refuse* to speak at the ceremony.　　27. _____

28. Neither the officer nor the spectators (1)*was* (2)*were* certain of the robber's identity.　　28. _____

29. Economics (1)*has* (2)*have* been the most dismal science I've ever studied.　　29. _____

30. (1)*Has* (2)*Have* either of the editorials appeared in the student newspaper?　　30. _____

31. It (1)**was** (2)**were** Arnold and Elise who came to see us yesterday while we were away. 31. _____

32. Neither Janet nor her parents (1)**seems** (2)**seem** interested in our offer to help. 32. _____

33. He is one of those fishers who habitually (1)**exaggerates** (2)**exaggerate** the size of the fish caught. 33. _____

30. GRAMMAR: AGREEMENT—PRONOUN AND ANTECEDENT

(Study G-9.2.)

Write the number of the **correct** choice.

Example: One of the riders fell off (1)*his* (2)*their* horse.   _____1_____

1. Agatha Christie is the kind of writer who loves to keep (1)*her* (2)*their* readers guessing until the last page.   1. _____

2. Vacationers flock to Hawaii because (1)*you* (2)*they* enjoy its awesome scenery and delightful climate.   2. _____

3. If anyone has found my wallet, will (1)*he* (2)*they* please return it.   3. _____

4. He majored in mathematics because (1)*it* (2)*they* had always been of interest to him.   4. _____

5. She presented extensive data, though (1)*it* (2)*they* had been difficult to assemble.   5. _____

6. He assumed that every student had done (1)*his* (2)*their* best to complete the test.   6. _____

7. Both Eddie and David decided to stretch (1)*his* (2)*their* legs when the bus reached Cornwall.   7. _____

8. Neither of the women had ever mentioned (1)*her* (2)*their* difficulties.   8. _____

9. Each of the attorneys spent several hours outlining (1)*his* (2)*their* ideas.   9. _____

10. He buys his books at the campus bookstore because (1)*it has* (2)*they have* low prices.   10. _____

11. Neither the president nor the deans had indicated (1)*her* (2)*their* position.   11. _____

12. Every member of the ski team received (1)*her* (2)*their* individual trophy.   12. _____

13. Our family made (1)*its* (2)*their* decision to spend less on Christmas this year.   13. _____

14. The jury seemed to be having difficulty in making up (1)*its mind* (2)*their minds.*   14. _____

15. Neither Margaret nor Ellen has paid (1)*her* (2)*their* dues yet.   15. _____

16. Anyone who doesn't turn in (1)*her* (2)*their* uniform will have to pay for it.   16. _____

17. Before someone can choose a career rationally, (1)*he* (2)*they* must have sufficient information. 17. _____

18. Neither the guide nor the hikers seemed aware of (1)*his or her* (2)*their* danger.   18. _____

19. The faculty has already made (1)*its* (2)*their* recommendations.   19. _____

20. I don't know what people see in (1)*those kind* (2)*those kinds* of movies.   20. _____

21. One has to decide early in life what (1)*he* (2)*they* can succeed at.   21. _____

22. Neither the coach nor the players underestimated (1)*his or her* (2)*their* opponents.   22. _____

23. Stan and the stage crew did (1)*his* (2)*their* best to complete the set on time.   23. _____

24. Both the pilot and the copilot thought that (1)*his* (2)*their* hour had come.   24. _____

25. Neither the Jays nor the Expos (1)*is* (2)*are* likely to win the pennant this year.   25. _____

26. In the London subway, riders pay according to the distance (1)*you* (2)*they* travel.   26. _____

27. If a stranger tried to talk to her, she would just look at (1)*him* (2)*them* and smile.   27. _____

28. Every one of the trees in the affected areas had lost most of (1)*its* (2)*their* leaves.   28. _____

29. A woman can understand (1)**herself** (2)**themself** (3)**themselves** better through reading feminist literature.   29. _____

30. The family seemed determined to go (1)**its** (2)**their** separate ways.   30. _____

31. The board of directors doesn't know what (1)**it's** (2)**they're** doing.   31. _____

32. No one should blame (1)**himself** (2)**themself** (3)**themselves** (4)**yourself** for misfortunes that cannot be prevented.   32. _____

33. Rita is one of those people who cannot control (1)**her** (2)**their** anger under stress.   33. _____

31. GRAMMAR: AGREEMENT—REVIEW

(Study G-9.)

Write **1** if the sentence is **correct** in agreement.
Write **0** if it is **incorrect**.

Example: Nobody in the first two rows are singing.	0
1. The deep blue of the waters seem to reflect the sky.	1. _____
2. Actors in a Tremblay play are exhausted by the final curtain.	2. _____
3. The survival chances of the prisoners in the Nazi camp were slim.	3. _____
4. The strength of these new space age materials have been demonstrated many times.	4. _____
5. All these experiences, along with the special love and care that my daughter needs, have taught me the value of caring.	5. _____
6. My main reason are the three papers I have due tomorrow.	6. _____
7. Does the six-thirty bus and the eight-o'clock train arrive in Hamilton before midnight?	7. _____
8. We teach every woman that there is nothing they cannot do as well as a man.	8. _____
9. The management now turned to its last resort: they asked the federal government for help with their financial problems.	9. _____
10. When a student first passes through the great gold gates of Kicking Horse College, he feels a thrill of expectation.	10. _____
11. I found that this thrill of expectation soon leaves when you have to visit the registrar's office.	11. _____
12. Everyone who heard the bombs declared that they had never before been so frightened.	12. _____
13. You should hire one of those experts who solves problems with computers.	13. _____
14. You should hire one of those kinds of experts who solve problems with computers.	14. _____
15. In our home, there were constant fighting and financial difficulty.	15. _____
16. Vancouver or Calgary is going to win the Grey Cup this year.	16. _____
17. Scotch and soda gives me heartburn if I use too much ice.	17. _____
18. Probably everybody in the dormitory except Penelope and Flora know what happened.	18. _____
19. Neither Chuck nor Arnold are as blessed with talent as Sylvester.	19. _____
20. The management has decided that they will not sell anyone a ticket until the theater opens its doors at noon.	20. _____

32. GRAMMAR: FRAGMENTS

(Study G-10.2A.)

Write **1** if the boldface words are a **complete sentence**.
Write **0** if they are a **fragment**.

Example: Martin was famished. *Having eaten only four hot dogs at the game.* ___0___

1. The lights flickered and went out. ***When the storm struck the coast.*** The blackout lasted for hours. 1. _____

2. ***Having applied for dozens of jobs and not having had any offers.*** 2. _____

3. ***The manuscript having been returned, Johanna sat down to revise it.*** 3. _____

4. Harrison desperately wanted the part. ***Because he believed that this was the film that would make him a star.*** 4. _____

5. ***Books, cameras, suitcases, blankets—all of which were piled on the porch.*** 5. _____

6. She was happy. ***As a matter of fact, she was delighted.*** 6. _____

7. ***The reason for the delay being that we had had a flat tire.*** 7. _____

8. She parked her car. ***Then she hurried into the courthouse.*** 8. _____

9. I have the latest news bulletin. ***Are you interested in hearing it?*** 9. _____

10. Maurice kept nodding his head as the coach explained the play. ***Thinking all the time that it would never work.*** 10. _____

11. ***Because she was interested in rocks, she majored in geology.*** 11. _____

12. I argued with two of my fellow students. ***First with Edward and then with Henry.*** 12. _____

13. Jackson made some bad investments. ***Such as buying desert land and speculating in cocoa beans.*** 13. _____

14. Taylor was absolutely positive he would pass. ***Regardless of having received failing grades on both his essay and the midterm.*** 14. _____

15. ***Colleen stepped up to the free-throw line; then she made two points to win the game.*** 15. _____

16. ***His term paper having been returned.*** He looked eagerly for the instructor's grade. 16. _____

17. ***Because he never fully realized how important a college education could be.*** 17. _____

18. She went to the supermarket. ***After she had made a list of groceries that she needed.*** 18. _____

19. Two hours before the contest, he was very nervous. ***Later, he felt very confident.*** 19. _____

20. I telephoned Dr. Gross. ***The man who had been our family physician for many years.*** 20. _____

21. We suspect Atterley of the theft. ***Because he had access to the funds and he has been living far beyond his means.*** 21. _____

22. He likes strawberry shortcake. ***Especially when it is topped with whipped cream.*** 22. _____

23. Please don't go. ***Stay.*** 23. _____

24. She is a star athlete. ***Besides being a brilliant student.*** 24. _____

25. I offered her a ticket to *Aïda.* ***An opera she had wanted to see.*** 25. _____

26. I planned to spend the summer with Uncle Henry. ***My father's youngest brother.*** 26. _____

27. ***Knowing that her time was limited, she took a taxi to the station.***   27. _____

28. My leg was in a cast for six months. ***To walk was difficult and painful.*** I became quite depressed.   28. _____

29. I was, however, determined. ***To make my leg as strong as ever.*** Strenuous daily exercises became
    my regimen.   29. _____

30. Harry Jerome never received the credit he deserved. ***Despite breaking the world record for the
    hundred meters.***   30. _____

33. GRAMMAR: COMMA SPLICES AND FUSED SENTENCES

(Study G-10.2B.)

Write **1** for each item that is a **single complete sentence.**
Write **0** for each item that is a **comma splice** or **fused sentence.**

Example: The mission was a success, everyone was pleased. _____0_____

1. The critics unanimously agreed the play was terrible it closed after a week. 1. _____

2. The party broke up at one in the morning, Ichabod lingered for a few final words with Katrina. 2. _____

3. *Intertidal Life* is about friendship and marriage; it is also about the difference between love and passion. 3. _____

4. In this essay, Frye deals with the English, French, and immigrant communities, his topic is the Canadian mosaic. 4. _____

5. Determined to sweep Atlantic Canada, the Prime Minister authorized extra campaign money to be spent there. 5. _____

6. If the moon enters the earth's shadow, a lunar eclipse occurs, which causes the moon to turn a deep red. 6. _____

7. Say hello to Wendell, if you see him, it's been weeks since he's been here. 7. _____

8. The ticket agent had sold eighty-one tickets to boarding passengers, yet there were only eleven empty seats on the train. 8. _____

9. When I saw what he had done, I couldn't believe my eyes he had repainted the whole room while I was gone. 9. _____

10. The film ended; no one noticed. 10. _____

11. The course was not so difficult as I had thought I earned an A. 11. _____

12. Since she did not believe that humankind's destiny was determined by forces beyond its control, she insisted that people were their own greatest enemies. 12. _____

13. Sheer exhaustion having caught up with me, I had no trouble falling asleep. 13. _____

14. As the music began, Ichabod arose and asked Katrina for a dance. 14. _____

15. The restaurant check almost made me faint, because I had left my wallet home, I couldn't pay for the meal. 15. _____

16. Those of us who owned cars ignored the rule, since we were about to graduate, we never worried about campus regulations. 16. _____

17. It was a cloudy, sultry afternoon when we sighted our first school of whales, and the cry of "Lower the boats!" rang throughout the ship. 17. _____

18. During the mating dance the female rats would come out of their burrows unexpectedly the males would stop dancing as the population increased. 18. _____

19. Now the war was over; however, nothing really could be done, the refugees could not be reunited with relatives who had come here earlier. 19. _____

20. They didn't try to fix the car, they just abandoned it. 20. _____

34. GRAMMAR: FRAGMENTS, COMMA SPLICES, AND FUSED SENTENCES

(Study G-10.2.)

Write **1** for each item that is a **complete sentence.**
Write **0** for each item that is a **fragment.**

Example: A man who neither seeks out trouble nor avoids it.   __0__

1. Because pie, ice cream, and candy bars have practically no nutritional value.   1. _____

2. When the bindings release, the ski comes off.   2. _____

3. Which was what the trade negotiators had wanted in the first place.   3. _____

4. The people Pearson worked with, who all knew him intimately.   4. _____

5. Whereas older cars run on regular gas and lack complex pollution controls.   5. _____

6. This was what the trade negotiators had wanted in the first place.   6. _____

7. If nothing had come of it, she would have been safe.   7. _____

8. If nothing had come of it, her safety in the workplace being fully assured by an employee benefits
   contract.   8. _____

9. Which could in no way be rationally explained by any of the scientists.   9. _____

10. Wait.   10. _____

Write **1** for each item that is **one or more complete, correct sentences.**
Write **2** for each item that contains a **fragment.**
Write **3** for each item that contains a **comma splice** or **fused sentence.**

Example: Today is Monday, tomorrow is Tuesday.   __3__

1. Clyde Griffiths' parents lacked the strength or wisdom to bring up their family properly. Clyde grew
   ashamed of his parents, his clothes, and his ugly surroundings.   1. _____

2. Clyde grew older, he dreamed of a life of wealth and elegance.   2. _____

3. He spent most of his meager earnings on clothes and luxuries for himself. Contributing little to his
   parents.   3. _____

4. Clyde managed to impress his wealthy uncle. Who gave him a job at his factory.   4. _____

5. One night Clyde's uncle invited him to a dinner. There he saw wealthy, beautiful Sondra Finchley.   5. _____

6. He became determined to have her, although she was too far above his social position, she lived in
   elegance.   6. _____

7. Clyde then started going with a factory girl named Roberta; she soon became pregnant by him.   7. _____

8. Sondra, growing to like Clyde, agreed to marry him, this made him see his dreams of wealth and status
   coming true.   8. _____

9. Meanwhile, Roberta expected Clyde to marry her, and Clyde knew. That if he had to marry her, his
   dreams would be ruined.   9. _____

10. Remembering a newspaper article about a young woman who had drowned in a rowboat accident,
    he invited Roberta to go rowing.   10. _____

11. What happened to German prisoners of war after World War II is told in the book *Other Losses* it was written by James Bacque.   11. _____

12. He wore a pair of mud-encrusted, flap-soled boots they looked older than he was.   12. _____

13. He wore a pair of mud-encrusted, flap-soled boots, footgear that looked older than he was.   13. _____

14. The computer produced pages of statistics, for the agency wanted to know how its money was spent.   14. _____

15. Dino reread his assignment a dozen times before handing it in. To be absolutely sure his ideas were clear.   15. _____

16. The representatives decided, however, to wait for the foreign minister's arrival before making a decision.   16. _____

17. That she is dead is beyond dispute.   17. _____

18. "I believe," declared the headmaster. "That you deserve expulsion."   18. _____

19. The scouts hiked two miles until they reached the falls, then they had lunch.   19. _____

20. The police having been warned to expect trouble, every available officer lined the avenue of the march.   20. _____

21. A still greater challenge faced them, it seemed impossible to warn the fort in time.   21. _____

22. Ireland's vital crop had been wiped out by the potato blight, nevertheless, Irish people who owned ten acres of land were disqualified from poor relief.   22. _____

23. The Irish immigrants to Canada did not go into farming for fear that the potato blight would strike there, but the German immigrants did go into farming, they had no fear of this blight.   23. _____

35. GRAMMAR: SENTENCE EFFECTIVENESS

(Study G-10.)

For each **correct** sentence, write **1.**
For each **incorrect** (ineffective) sentence, write the number that **explains** the error:

2. **failure to subordinate details**
3. **childishly choppy sentences**
4. **overuse of** *and*
5. **needless separation of subject and verb or parts of infinitive**
6. **dangling, misplaced, or squinting modifier**

7. **nonparallel structure**
8. **omission in comparison or degree**
9. **shift in person, number, tense, voice, etc.**
10. **redundancy (including double negative and superfluous** *that***)**
11. **inflated phrasing**

Example: He wanted *to shower* and *to sleep*.	1
Example: That was a *most unique* moment.	10

1. If *one* drives a car without thinking, *you* are more than likely to have an accident. 1. _____

2. She said *that,* if I helped her with her math, *that* she would type my paper. 2. _____

3. The entire class was *so* pleased at learning that Dr. Turner had rescheduled the quiz. 3. _____

4. I intended to *carefully and thoughtfully* consider my program for the fall term. 4. _____

5. The director, thinking *only* about how he could get the shot of the exploding car, endangered everyone. 5. _____

6. She *could hardly* hear the speaker because of the noise in the hallway. 6. _____

7. *Looking down from the top of the hill,* the houses appeared to be very small. 7. _____

8. The children learned *to dance* and *singing.* 8. _____

9. She *walks* onto the platform, and then she *began* to speak quietly to the audience. 9. _____

10. He *couldn't hardly* make himself heard because of the noise outside. 10. _____

11. She sat down *and* opened her purse *and* took out her pen *and* began to write. 11. _____

12. He told me *that he was going to write a letter* and *not to disturb him.* 12. _____

13. *Eleanor Gruen is an English major,* and she just won national recognition for her poetry. 13. _____

14. Mike *baked* a cake, and much time *was spent* in frosting it. 14. _____

15. If a *student* knows how to study, *he* should achieve academic success. 15. _____

16. *He went to his office. He sat down. He opened his briefcase. He read some papers.* 16. _____

17. Summer is a time for *parties, friendships, for athletics,* and *in which we can relax.* 17. _____

18. Juliet and I must *make a decision, within one passage of the sun across the heavens, as to whether we should be forever united in holy wedlock.* 18. _____

19. He is *such* a great goalie! 19. _____

20. I shot a bear *in my pajamas.* 20. _____

21. Being a ski jumper requires *nerves of steel, you have to concentrate to the utmost,* and *being perfectly coordinated.* 21. _____

22. ***The situation in regard to decisions on the possible expenditure of my monetary resources is such that any commitment on my part to such expenditure must be considered with extreme caution.***   22. _____

23. The plane neither had ***enough fuel*** nor ***proper radar equipment.***   23. _____

24. ***My personal opinion is that I think that*** the Expos will win their division by ten games.   24. _____

25. The malfunctioning landing gear ***killed nearly*** everyone on the plane; only one person survived.   25. _____

Write the number of the **most effective** way of expressing the given ideas.

Example: 1. At this moment in time, I regret that it was impossible for me to partake in my morning repast.
2. I had to skip breakfast.
3. I had not hardly enough time for breakfast.   ____2____

1. 1. We found a little Hungarian restaurant. It was on Sherbrooke Street. We went in it to eat.
   2. We went to eat at a little Hungarian restaurant that we found on Sherbrooke Street.
   3. There was a little Hungarian restaurant on Sherbrooke Street, and we found it there and went in to eat.   1. _____

2. 1. The house that my mother bought was located between two gasoline stations.
   2. The house that my mother bought was located where there was a gasoline station on one side of it and another gasoline station on the other side.
   3. The domicile purchased by my maternal parent was juxtaposed to automotive refueling establishments on either side.   2. _____

3. 1. The terrorists revealed the condition of their hostages well after they demanded food and fuel.
   2. The terrorists wanted food. They wanted the plane refueled. Until then, they didn't reveal the condition of their hostages.
   3. Before revealing the condition of their hostages, the terrorists demanded fuel and food.   3. _____

4. 1. Harry, who woke up in the morning to find his car wouldn't start, had forgotten to plug in the block heater.
   2. Harry, who had forgotten to plug in the block heater, woke up in the morning to find his car wouldn't start.
   3. Harry had forgotten to plug in the block heater, and he woke up in the morning to find his car wouldn't start.   4. _____

5. 1. The papers were marked *top secret.* The term *top secret* indicates contents of extraordinary value.
   2. The papers were of extraordinary value, and therefore they were marked *top secret.*
   3. The papers were marked *top secret,* indicating their extraordinary value.   5. _____

36. GRAMMAR: PARALLEL STRUCTURE

(Study G-10.1F.)

Write **1** if the boldface words or word groups are **all in parallel structure.**
Write **0** if the boldface words or word groups are **not all in parallel structure.**

Example: Lilliputian politicians practiced *leaping* and *creeping.*   1

1. Audrey impressed everyone by her *wit, charm, grace,* and *intelligence.*   1. _____

2. J.R. *put three competitors into bankruptcy, lied to his wife and brother,* and then *his breakfast was brought to him.*   2. _____

3. The apartment could be rented *by the week, by the month,* or *you could pay on a yearly basis.*   3. _____

4. *What I saw, what I did,* and *what I endured* during those tragic days will always haunt my memory.   4. _____

5. Our new wood-burning stove *should keep us warm, save us money,* and *should afford us much pleasure.*   5. _____

6. *Where my father went on Friday nights, what he did there,* and *how much of the family's money he wasted on those occasions,* I never found out until years later.   6. _____

7. Our family Bible is *old, beautiful,* and *has been read by many.*   7. _____

8. The chief ordered agent 007 *to break into the building, crack the safe,* and *to steal the atomic yo-yo plans.*   8. _____

9. Barbara likes especially to *read Tolstoy, sketch landscapes,* and *run in marathons.*   9. _____

10. Losing *his wife to death, his self-control to liquor,* and *the loss of his daughter's custody* brought Charlie to the brink of despair.   10. _____

Write **1** if the sentence **contains parallel structure.**
Write **0** if the sentence **violates parallel structure.**

Example: The candidates took lessons in how to kiss babies and looking honest.   0

1. I knew what I was supposed to do but not when I was supposed to do it or how I could accomplish it.   1. _____

2. The scouts marched briskly off into the woods, trekked ten miles to Alder Lake, and tents were erected by them.   2. _____

3. Rodney, the hero of the novel, had three main characteristics: his ambition, he hated von Stroeblicht, and his love for Maria.   3. _____

4. Charles liked both painting and operatic singing.   4. _____

5. Charles liked not only painting but also to sing opera.   5. _____

6. I learned my French at school, at home, and where I work.   6. _____

7. The dance committee members realized that they had to either raise the ticket price or find a smaller band.   7. _____

8. Neither regulating prices nor wages will slow inflation enough.   8. _____

9. Tightening the money supply is more effective than if taxes are raised.   9. _____

10. Mick practiced shooting from the top of the key as well as how to dribble with either hand.   10. _____

37. GRAMMAR: PARALLEL STRUCTURE

(Study G-10.1F.)

Write **1** if the bold words or word groups are **all in parallel structure;** write **0** if they are not.
Then, in the last three columns, identify each element as follows:

2. noun (including gerunds)
3. participial
4. verb phrase (with or without complement)
5. prepositional phrase
6. infinitive
7. clause
8. adjective

	Parallel	#1	#2	#3
Example: Grandmother insisted on *cleanliness, godliness, and being prompt.*	0	2	2	3
1. Bobby was always *laughing, smiling, and joking.*	1. _____	___	___	___
2. Hector fought *with great skill, with epic daring, and superb intelligence.*	2. _____	___	___	___
3. The credo Tennyson's Ulysses cherished was *to strive, to seek, and not yield.*	3. _____	___	___	___
4. The castle was *built on a hill, surrounded by farmland, and commanded a magnificent view.*	4. _____	___	___	___
5. Walker can *throw, hit, and he is a good base stealer.*	5. _____	___	___	___
6. By nightfall, *we were tired, we were hungry, and homesick.*	6. _____	___	___	___
7. The guerrillas *surrounded the village, set up their mortars, and the shelling began.*	7. _____	___	___	___
8. Orlando did not know *where she had come from, why she was there, or the time of her departure.*	8. _____	___	___	___
9. Her favorite pastimes remain *designing clothes, cooking gourmet meals, and practicing the flute.*	9. _____	___	___	___
10. Eliot's poetry is *witty, complex, and draws on his vast learning.*	10. _____	___	___	___

38. GRAMMAR: PLACEMENT OF MODIFIERS

(Study G-10.2C, D.)

Write **1** if the boldface word(s) are **correctly** placed.
Write **0** if the boldface word(s) are **incorrectly** placed.

Example: Never give a toy to a child *which can be swallowed.*   0

1. He ordered a pizza for his friends *covered with pepperoni.*   1. _____
2. Mr. Andrus spotted a bird sitting on a telephone wire *that he could not identify.*   2. _____
3. She had enough money to buy *only* two of the three books that she needed.   3. _____
4. She saw a police officer on a horse, *looking out our fifth-floor window one day.*   4. _____
5. We knew that to *quickly and thoroughly* cleanse the wound was necessary.   5. _____
6. We saw the plane taxi onto the field *that would soon be leaving for St. John.*   6. _____
7. The Larsons were spending *almost* a third of their income on rent.   7. _____
8. Derek found a clue in his bedroom *that he had never seen before.*   8. _____
9. In the basement of the store, we found a sale of *soiled* women's purses.   9. _____
10. We hurriedly bought a picnic table from a clerk *with collapsible legs.*   10. _____
11. We learned that no one could discard anything at the municipal dump *except people living in the community.*   11. _____
12. We had trouble finding a *red, white, and blue* child's violin for the show.   12. _____
13. Although he has tried several times, he just can't learn to drive a car *with a standard shift.*   13. _____
14. The bride walked down the aisle with her father *wearing her mother's wedding gown.* 14. _____
15. Despite his best intentions, he failed to *over the years* return home for Christmas. 15. _____
16. Naomi's grandfather lived to be *nearly* ninety years old.   16. _____
17. "This is the best book I *almost* ever read!" she exclaimed.   17. _____
18. Call, *after you have addressed these 106 envelopes,* me at home.   18. _____
19. *Only* one teacher seems able to convince Raymond that he should study.   19. _____
20. She loved the meal prepared for her by her husband *in the microwave.*   20. _____
21. I had considered *for several days* the possibility of eloping.   21. _____
22. We watched the *QE II* as she slowly sailed out to sea *from our hotel window.*   22. _____
23. Indicate *on the enclosed mimeographed sheet* whether you are going to the class picnic.   23. _____
24. A *battered* man's hat was hanging on a branch of the tree.   24. _____
25. He found a pie baked by his wife *on the top shelf of the refrigerator.*   25. _____
26. She found the wedding dress worn by her mother *hanging in the attic.*   26. _____
27. He gave the scraps of meat to the dog *that had been left on the dinner plates.*   27. _____
28. Marcel Dionne said *when he scored his two-thousandth point* he would retire.   28. _____
29. Mary Bell had decided *before her son was two years old* that the boy would be a lawyer.   29. _____
30. He replied *usually* they went to Paris in the spring.   30. _____

39. GRAMMAR: DANGLING MODIFIERS

(Study G-10.2D.)

Write **1** if the boldface words are used **correctly.**
Write **0** if they are used **incorrectly** (**dangling**).

Example: *Dancing to stardom,* fame is an elusive goal.	0
1. *Dreaming of seeing her name in lights,* Wendy bought a bus ticket to New York.	1. _____
2. *Rowing across the lake,* the moon often disappeared behind the clouds.	2. _____
3. *Having walked three miles,* the cabin was a welcome sight to all of us.	3. _____
4. *While shaving,* the idea for a new play came to him.	4. _____
5. *Trapped alone there at midnight,* the house creaked and moaned with every step.	5. _____
6. *After roasting for five hours at 325°,* you will have a delicious turkey.	6. _____
7. *Upon entering college,* he applied for part-time employment in the library.	7. _____
8. *When a little girl,* my brother threw a rock at me.	8. _____
9. *To get to Carnegie Hall,* practice must go on for hours every day.	9. _____
10. *To assure a good catch,* the fish should find a fresh, juicy worm on your hook.	10. _____
11. *After waiting for an hour,* word reached us that the speaker had been delayed.	11. _____
12. *When nine years old,* my father took my brother and me on our first camping trip.	12. _____
13. *At the age of ten,* I was permitted to go, for the first time, to a summer camp.	13. _____
14. *After putting away my fishing equipment,* the surface of the lake became choppy.	14. _____
15. *While visiting the zoo,* the chimpanzees entertained the children.	15. _____
16. *To achieve a goal,* a person must expect to work and to make sacrifices.	16. _____
17. *Hanging on a nail in the clothes closet,* my neighbor's plaid jacket had lost its shape.	17. _____
18. *After hearing of Tom's need for financial aid,* a hundred dollars was put at his disposal.	18. _____
19. *To unroll and lay linoleum successfully,* the room must be reasonably warm.	19. _____
20. *Pickled in spiced vinegar,* the host thought the peaches would go with the meat.	20. _____
21. *While reaching for a hammer,* the ladder began to tip.	21. _____
22. *Disappointed at the poor attendance,* the play closed Saturday night.	22. _____
23. *By saving his money for two years,* Arthur was able to finance his trip to Europe.	23. _____
24. *After being cleaned and wrapped in waxed paper,* the fisher put the day's catch in the freezer.	24. _____
25. *Discovering that I had left my wallet at home,* I asked Janet to pay for our lunch.	25. _____
26. *As an infant,* Darlene was up every night at four to feed Emma.	26. _____
27. *Getting up early,* the house seemed unusually quiet to me.	27. _____
28. Finally, *after working for days,* the garden was free of weeds.	28. _____
29. *To receive a reply to your question,* a self-addressed envelope is needed.	29. _____
30. *After finishing my assignment,* the dog ate it.	30. _____

40. GRAMMAR: DANGLING MODIFIERS

(Study G-10.2D.)

Write **1** if the boldface words are used **correctly.**
Write **0** if the boldface words are used **incorrectly.**
In the second column, write the word to which the boldface words **now refer.**

Example: *After dancing the lead in* **Swan Lake,** cheers filled the hall.   <u> 0 </u>   <u> cheers </u>

1. *Writing during the Renaissance,* poems were characterized as speaking pictures.   1. ___ _____

2. *Approaching Toronto,* the view of the skyline was exciting.   2. ___ _____

3. *To have a just society,* discrimination in all forms must disappear.   3. ___ _____

4. *After looking all over the house,* my wallet turned up on my night table.   4. ___ _____

5. *Before spending a dollar,* Granny always thought twice.   5. ___ _____

6. *Angered by his conversation with the Boy Wonder,* Duddy began to plot his revenge.   6. ___ _____

7. *To get a passing grade in this course,* the professor's little quirks must be considered.   7. ___ _____

8. *Sleeping until noon each day,* the sunlight shining through the window wouldn't wake me.   8. ___ _____

9. *While raging against the storm,* King Lear learned of humanity's suffering.   9. ___ _____

10. *Having read the morning paper,* it was tossed aside.   10. ___ _____

41. GRAMMAR: REVIEW

(Study G.)

Write **1** for each statement that is **true**.
Write **0** for each that is **false**.

Example: A *present participle* is a word that ends in *-ing* and is used as an adjective.   ___1___

1. Both a *gerund* and a *present participle* end in *-ing*.   1. _____

2. The greatest number of words ever used in a *verb* is four.   2. _____

3. *Parallel structure* is used to designate ideas that are not equal in importance.   3. _____

4. A *dangling participle* may be corrected by being changed into a dependent clause.   4. _____

5. *It's* is a *contraction* of *it is*; *its* is the *possessive form* of the pronoun *it*.   5. _____

6. The *predicate precedes the subject* in a sentence beginning with the expletive *there*.   6. _____

7. A *preposition* may contain two or more words; *because of* is an example.   7. _____

8. The *principal parts of a verb* are the *present tense*, the *future tense*, and the *past participle*. 8. _____

9. A *collective noun* may be followed by either a singular or a plural verb.   9. _____

10. A *prepositional phrase* may be used only as an adjective modifier.   10. _____

11. A *compound sentence* is one that contains two or more independent clauses.   11. _____

12. Not all *adverbs* end in *-ly*.   12. _____

13. *To lie* is an *intransitive verb*; *to lay* is a *transitive verb* and is always followed by a direct object. 13. _____

14. A *noun clause* may be introduced by the subordinate conjunction *although*.   14. _____

15. An *adjective clause* may begin with *when* or *where*.   15. _____

16. Both *verbals* and *verbs* may have modifiers and complements.   16. _____

17. The terminal punctuation of a declarative sentence is the *exclamation point*.   17. _____

18. *Without* is a *subordinate conjunction.*   18. _____

19. A sentence beginning with *because* must have both a *dependent* and an *independent clause*.   19. _____

20. The *predicate* of a sentence cannot consist of merely a past participle.   20. _____

21. A *subjective complement* may be a noun, a pronoun, or an adverb.   21. _____

22. A *direct object* may be a noun or a pronoun.   22. _____

23. An *indirect object* always follows the direct object.   23. _____

24. An *objective complement* always precedes the direct object.   24. _____

25. The words *to be* or *to have been,* when preceded by a noun or pronoun, are followed by an *object pronoun*.   25. _____

26. The word *scissors* takes a *singular verb.*   26. _____

27. An *antecedent* is the noun for which a pronoun stands.   27. _____

28. A *simple sentence* contains two or more independent clauses.   28. _____

29. Pronouns in the *objective case* always follow forms of the verb *to be*.   29. _____

30. Joining two independent clauses with only the comma (a **comma splice**) is considered incorrect.   30. _____

31. A **sentence fragment** is not considered a legitimate unit of expression; a **nonsentence** is.   31. _____

32. **Adjectives** never stand next to the words they modify.   32. _____

33. Not all words ending in *-ly* are **adverbs.**   33. _____

34. An **indefinite pronoun** designates no particular person.   34. _____

35. The words *have* and *has* identify the **present perfect tense** of a verb.   35. _____

36. An **absolute phrase** consists essentially of a noun or a pronoun and a participle.   36. _____

37. An **adverb** may modify a noun, an adjective, or another adverb.   37. _____

38. **Verbs** are words that assert an action or a state of being.   38. _____

39. The **indicative mood** of a verb is used to express a command or a request.   39. _____

40. The function of a **subordinate conjunction** is to join a dependent clause to a main clause.   40. _____

41. A **predicate** need not agree in number with its subject.   41. _____

42. An **adjective** may modify a noun, a pronoun, or an adverb.   42. _____

43. A **gerund** is a word ending in *-ing* and used as a noun.   43. _____

44. A **clause** differs from a **phrase** in that a clause always has a subject and a predicate.   44. _____

45. **Adjectives** tell *what kind, how many,* or *which one;* **adverbs** tell *when, where, how,* and *to what degree.*   45. _____

46. **Pronouns ending in -self** (*himself, myself,* etc.) should not be substituted for **personal pronouns** (*he, me,* etc.).   46. _____

47. **Coordinate conjunctions** (*and, but, or, nor, for, yet*) join words, phrases, and clauses of equal importance.   47. _____

48. **Pronouns in the objective case** (*him, me,* etc.) should be used as direct objects of verbs and verbals.   48. _____

49. A **linking verb** agrees with its subjective complement.   49. _____

50. When a **subject** that is singular is joined to one that is plural by *or,* the verb agrees with the farther subject.   50. _____

Write **1** if the sentence is **correct.**
Write **0** if it is **incorrect.**

Example: Was that letter sent to Paul or *I*?   ___0___

1. **Having been notified to come at once,** there was no opportunity for me to call you.   1. _____

2. I suspected that his remarks were directed to Larry and **me.**   2. _____

3. He, **thinking that he might find his friends on the second floor of the library,** hurried.   3. _____

4. She refused to get into the sailboat **without** I went with her.   4. _____

5. In the cabin of the boat **was** a radio, a set of flares, and a map of the area.   5. _____

6. The Queen, standing beside her husband, children, and grandchildren, **were** waving regally at the crowd.   6. _____

7. She is a person **who** I think is certain to succeed as a social worker.   7. _____

8. **Is** there any other questions you wish to ask regarding the new sales tax?   8. _____

9. **Do** either of you know in which direction he went?   9. _____

10. He particularly enjoys **water skiing** and **to paddle** a canoe.   10. _____

11. Forward the complaint to **whoever** you think is in charge.   11. _____

12. He decided that every boy and girl **was** to have a ride on the merry-go-round.   12. _____

13. Neither the bus driver nor the passengers **were** aware of their danger.   13. _____

14. She **not only** likes you **but also** your whole family.   14. _____

15. What a pity that not everyone offers **their** help to feed the hungry.   15. _____

16. Homemade bread tastes **differently** from bakery bread.   16. _____

17. **Not having had the chance to consult his lawyer,** it was impossible for him to remember his mother's name.   17. _____

18. **Is** either of your friends interested in watching a television program with me?   18. _____

19. He enrolled in economics because **it** had always been of interest to him.   19. _____

20. Jacob read **steady** for two weeks before he finished the novel.   20. _____

21. Burt paced nervously up and down the corridor. **Because Howard had never been this late before.**   21. _____

22. **A heavy rain began without warning, the crew struggled with the tarpaulin.**   22. _____

23. To take a good picture, **the light must not be too bright.**   23. _____

24. Casey asked for time, stepped out of the batter's box, **and his finger was pointed toward the bleachers.**   24. _____

25. The jury could not make up **its** mind about Marshall's guilt.   25. _____

42. PUNCTUATION: THE COMMA

(Study P-1.)

If **no comma** is needed in the bracketed space(s), write **0** in the blank at the right.

If **one or more commas** are needed, write in the blank the number (**1 to 10** from the list below) of the **reason** for the comma(s).

(Use only one number in each blank.)

1. **independent clauses joined by** *and, but, or, nor, for, yet*
2. **introductory adverb clause**
3. **series**
4. **parenthetical expression (other than nonrestrictive clause)**
5. **nonrestrictive clause**

6. **appositive**
7. **absolute phrase**
8. **direct address**
9. **mild interjection**
10. **direct quotation**

Example: Donald's nephews are Huey[ ] Dewey[ ] and Louie.   3

1. *Dance on the Earth*[ ] Margaret Laurence's memoirs[ ] traces her life and writing career in Canada, Africa, and England.   1. _____

2. Any professor[ ] who assigns long papers[ ] will have small classes.   2. _____

3. Well[ ] I guess we'll have to leave without Ida.   3. _____

4. If there are no other questions[ ] let's begin our game.   4. _____

5. So you see[ ] Dr. Haywood[ ] I can't possibly pay your bill by next week.   5. _____

6. Phillip's father[ ] who is a conservative gentleman[ ] disapproves of teenage antics.   6. _____

7. Roy and Trigger[ ] however[ ] were waiting back at the ranch.   7. _____

8. John Fitzgerald Kennedy[ ] the thirty-fifth President of the United States[ ] was assassinated on November 22, 1963.   8. _____

9. I left early for the game[ ] my friends having warned me about the heavy traffic.   9. _____

10. Before she was able to pick up the receiver[ ] the telephone had stopped ringing.   10. _____

11. He sat down at his desk last evening[ ] and made a preliminary draft of his speech.   11. _____

12. Julie went into the library[ ] but she hurried out a few minutes later.   12. _____

13. Diefenbaker laughed at the Grits[ ] dismissed the NDP[ ] and exalted the Tories.   13. _____

14. After she had watched her favorite television program[ ] she settled down to study.   14. _____

15. The candidate gave a number of speeches in Perth[ ] where she hoped to win support.   15. _____

16. She has always wanted to visit the small village[ ] where her father had lived.   16. _____

17. My instructor[ ] Professor Ursula Tyler[ ] outlined the work for the current semester.   17. _____

18. If I forget thee[ ] O Jerusalem[ ] let my right hand forget her cunning.   18. _____

19. "Is this[ ]" she asked[ ] "the only excuse that you have to offer?"   19. _____

20. Canada has never been a melting pot[ ] Arnold Edinborough remarked[ ] as much as a tossed salad.   20. _____

21. Her guests having finally left[ ] she opened her books and began to study.   21. _____

22. Joyce became a doctor[ ] and Claude became a laboratory technician.   22. _____

23. Oh[ ] I had no idea that you would be offended by my frivolous remarks.   23. _____

24. We were asked to read *Lady Oracle*[ ] which is a novel by Margaret Atwood.   24. _____

25. Stephen Leacock[ ] the author of *Sunshine Sketches of a Little Town*[ ] created the fictional town of Mariposa.   25. _____

43. PUNCTUATION: THE COMMA

(Study P-1.)

If **no comma** is needed in the bracketed space(s), write **0** in the blank at the right.
If **one or more commas** are needed, write in the blank the number (**1** to **10** from the list below) of the **reason** for the comma(s).
(Use only one number in each blank.)

1. parenthetical expression (other than nonrestrictive clause)
2. nonrestrictive clause
3. direct address
4. after *yes* or *no*
5. before *such as, especially,* or *particularly*
6. contrast
7. omission
8. confirmatory question
9. date
10. state or country

Example: The Allies invaded Normandy on June 6[ ] 1944.   ___9___

1. Our house[ ] which had stood since 1901[ ] burned to the ground.   1. _____

2. Prime Minister[ ] would you comment on reports that you will not run again?   2. _____

3. Ottawa[ ] Ontario[ ] was Wendy's home.   3. _____

4. You would like more pie[ ] wouldn't you?   4. _____

5. You will agree[ ] of course[ ] with the board's decision.   5. _____

6. I hope[ ] Charles and Mary[ ] that you will come to see us often.   6. _____

7. The person[ ] who did that to you[ ] should go to prison.   7. _____

8. For dessert, John ordered strawberry shortcake; Louise[ ] pineapple sherbert.   8. _____

9. Is it true[ ] sir[ ] that you are unwilling to be interviewed by the press?   9. _____

10. Our next contestant comes all the way from Napanee[ ] Ontario[ ] just to be with us today.   10. _____

11. Frank graduated from the University of Waterloo; Esther[ ] from Trent University.   11. _____

12. Students[ ] who work their way through college[ ] learn to value their college training.   12. _____

13. She said, "No[ ] I absolutely refuse to answer your question."   13. _____

14. Fat Albert loves all beautiful things[ ] particularly hamburgers and french fries.   14. _____

15. December 7[ ] 1941[ ] will be remembered as a day of infamy.   15. _____

16. I had wanted to see the janitor[ ] not the apartment-house manager.   16. _____

17. Nevertheless[ ] we were fortunate to have recovered a part of our luggage.   17. _____

18. The instructor told us to read the poem[ ] and to write our impressions of it.   18. _____

19. You are expecting to spend the evening with us[ ] aren't you?   19. _____

20. I've already told you[ ] little boy[ ] that I'm not giving you back your ball.   20. _____

21. Lester Pearson[ ] who won the Nobel Peace Prize in 1956[ ] was born in Newtonbrook, Ontario.   21. _____

22. Not everyone[ ] who objected to the new ruling[ ] signed the petition.   22. _____

23. It was[ ] on the other hand[ ] an opportunity that he could not turn down.   23. _____

24. Sir John A. Macdonald[ ] who was our first prime minister[ ] was born in 1815.   24. _____

25. She has several hobbies[ ] such as collecting coins, writing verse, and growing roses.   25. _____

44. PUNCTUATION: THE COMMA

(Study P-1.)

If **no comma** is needed in the bracketed space(s), write **0** in the blank at the right.
If **one or more commas** are needed, write in the blank the number (**1 to 11** from the list below) of the **reason** for the comma(s).
(Use only one number in each blank.)

1. independent clauses joined by *and, but, or, nor, for, yet*
2. introductory adverb clause
3. long introductory prepositional phrase
4. introductory participial phrase
5. introductory infinitive phrase
6. series

7. coordinate adjectives
8. appositive
9. absolute phrase
10. mild interjection
11. direct quotation

Example: James Joyce[ ] Ireland's most famous novelist[ ] lived most of his life abroad.   <u>   8   </u>

1. The BC Lions have good running backs[ ] and look good on defense as well.   1. _____

2. Well[ ] we'll probably see another foot of snow before the winter ends.   2. _____

3. Agatha Christie[ ] the famous mystery writer[ ] caricatured herself in her books.   3. _____

4. Appalled by the restaurant's prices[ ] Katharine vowed never to return.   4. _____

5. The concert having ended[ ] the fans rushed toward the stage.   5. _____

6. He hoped to write short stories[ ] publish his poems[ ] and plan a novel.   6. _____

7. If you wish to go to Victoria next spring[ ] I'll plan to go with you.   7. _____

8. Many people had tried to reach the top of the mountain[ ] but only a few had succeeded.   8. _____

9. Equipped with only an inexpensive camera[ ] she succeeded in taking a prize-winning picture.   9. _____

10. During times of emotional distress and heightened tensions[ ] Madeline remains calm.   10. _____

11. To gather pine cones for Christmas decorations[ ] he traveled far up the mountain.   11. _____

12. Recognizing that his position was hopeless[ ] Krilov resigned.   12. _____

13. That it was late[ ] and that we were tired was all too evident.   13. _____

14. Mr. Novak found himself surrounded by noisy[ ] exuberant students.   14. _____

15. "We are[ ]" she said[ ] "prepared to serve meals to a group of considerable size."   15. _____

16. Grace had no intention of withdrawing from college[ ] nor was she willing to carry a lighter program.   16. _____

17. To master the tuba[ ] one has to practice for years.   17. _____

18. Although storm clouds were gathering[ ] we made the trip across the lake in the kayak.   18. _____

19. "You must be more quiet[ ] or the landlord will make us move," she said.   19. _____

20. We asked Pat Barton[ ] the peewee coach[ ] to suggest a suitable hockey school.   20. _____

21. I could not decide whether to go to college[ ] or to go to Nigeria with my aunt.   21. _____

22. Built on a high cliff[ ] the house afforded a panoramic view of the valley below.   22. _____

23. The ringing of the telephone having awakened him[ ] he was unable to go back to sleep.   23. _____

24. The professor raised his voice to a shout[ ] the class having apparently dozed off.   24. _____

25. Her courses include Russian[ ] organic chemistry[ ] and marine biology.   25. _____

45. PUNCTUATION: THE COMMA

(Study P-1.)

In the blank,

> write **1** if the punctuation in brackets is **correct;**
> write **0** if it is **incorrect.**

(Use only one number in each blank.)

Example: We would appreciate it[,] therefore[,] if you paid your bill and left.	__1__
1. She died[,] because she had been unable to find shelter.	1. _____
2. We traveled to Québec[,] and went up the St. Lawrence River.	2. _____
3. "Tell me," he demanded[,] "who you are."	3. _____
4. When the results were in[,] the Tory candidate was the winner.	4. _____
5. You expect to graduate in June[,] don't you?	5. _____
6. O'Conner started the second half at linebacker[,] O'Hara having torn his knee ligaments.	6. _____
7. O'Conner started the second half at linebacker[,] O'Hara had torn his knee ligaments.	7. _____
8. Trying to concentrate[,] Susan closed the door and turned off the television set.	8. _____
9. "My fellow Kiwanians[,] this is a real opportunity to be of service," he said.	9. _____
10. Some of the older and more conservative members of the tennis club[,] did not approve of Roseanna's dress.	10. _____
11. Judy, who especially enjoys baseball, sat in the front row[,] and watched the game closely.	11. _____
12. "Are you going to a fire?"[,] the police officer asked the speeding motorist.	12. _____
13. Two of the students left the office[,] the third waited to see the dean.	13. _____
14. The coach and three of her players[,] recently appeared on a television program.	14. _____
15. "I won't wait any longer," she said[,] picking up her books from the bench.	15. _____
16. We looked down from our plane on the rugged[,] snow-covered mountains.	16. _____
17. The relatively short drought[,] nonetheless[,] had still caused much damage to the crops.	17. _____
18. The apartment they rented[,] had no screens or storm windows.	18. _____
19. I opened my presents[,] then I cut my birthday cake.	19. _____
20. However[,] much you may think you like ice cream, two quarts will be too much.	20. _____
21. In Milton, Ontario[,] on August 18, 1984, Shirley and Don were married.	21. _____
22. "Wait a minute," he said[,] "I have a matter that I wish to discuss with you."	22. _____
23. Her grandfather[,] who has trouble understanding young people today[,] frowned and left the room.	23. _____
24. Gabrielle Roy[,] the author of *The Tin Flute*[,] grew up in Manitoba.	24. _____
25. Next summer she hopes to fulfill a lifelong wish[,] to travel to the Arctic.	25. _____
26. Today let's just sit[,] talk[,] and rest; tomorrow we'll be very busy.	26. _____
27. Her last day in the office[,] was spent in sorting papers and filing manuscripts.	27. _____

28. To enable us to find you in an emergency[,] leave your telephone number at the desk. 28. _____

29. Having booted up her word processor[,] Colleen's quest for the Great Canadian Novel began. 29. _____

30. Haven't you any idea[,] of the responsibility involved in running a household? 30. _____

46. PUNCTUATION: THE COMMA

(Study P-1.)

If there should be **a comma** at any one or more of the numbered spaces in a sentence, circle the corresponding number(s) in the column at the right.

If there should be **no commas** in the sentence, circle **0.**

Example: I'll have a hamburger fries and a coke with lots of ice.   0 ①② 3 4
                                    1   2   3   4

1. Amanda bought paint a roller and two brushes.   1. 0 1 2 3
           1   2   3
2. Because Gulliver believed that all human beings were Yahoos he despised them.   2. 0 1 2 3 4
       1   2   3   4
3. Phil mixed the eggs onions and peppers before frying them.   3. 0 1 2 3 4
          1   2   3   4
4. And now my proud beauty you will do exactly what I say.   4. 0 1 2 3 4
        1   2   3   4
5. I wanted to go to Queen's; Terry to Simon Fraser.   5. 0 1 2 3
       1   2   3
6. No I know nothing regarding her whereabouts.   6. 0 1 2 3
      1   2   3
7. I phoned Jack this morning but he wasn't at home or at work.   7. 0 1 2 3 4
            1   2 3   4
8. The MP who had already served two terms in Parliament and one in the National Assembly
        1   2   3
   declared his candidacy again.   8. 0 1 2 3 4
             4
9. I was born on December 1 1965 in Estivan Saskatchewan during a blizzard.   9. 0 1 2 3 4
                      1   2   3   4
10. I consider him to be a hardworking student but I may be wrong.   10. 0 1 2 3 4
          1   2   3 4
11. Audrey a woman whom I met last summer is here to see me.   11. 0 1 2 3 4
        1   2   3   4
12. Having an interest in anthropology she frequently audited Dr. Irwin's class that met on Saturdays. 12. 0 1 2 3 4
             1   2   3   4
13. Her friends her relatives and her husband urged her to reconsider her decision to leave. 13. 0 1 2 3 4
           1   2   3   4
14. Well I dislike her intensely but she is quite clever to be sure.   14. 0 1 2 3 4
       1   2 3   4
15. To solve her legal problems she consulted a lawyer that she knew from college. 15. 0 1 2 3
                        1   2   3
16. "To what " he asked "do you attribute your great popularity with the students?" 16. 0 1 2 3 4
        1   2   3   4
17. Some of the specimens that you will see on display today were alive more than 100,000 years
                    1   2
    ago when the dinosaurs were masters of the earth.   17. 0 1 2 3 4
      3   4
18. *Heartbreak House* a comedy by George Bernard Shaw was produced at Niagara in the early
               1   2   3   4
    1980s.   18. 0 1 2 3 4

19. Boyd Staunton appeared to all the villagers to be a successful man; he was nonetheless deeply
                    1   2   3   4
    unhappy.   19. 0 1 2 3 4

20. "You haven't seen my glasses have you?" Granny asked the twins thinking they had hidden them
                                1   2   3   4
    in her tomato soup.   20. 0 1 2 3 4

21. The car having broken down because of a dirty carburetor we missed the first act in which Hamlet
                        1   2   3   4
    confronts his father's ghost.   21. 0 1 2 3 4

22. After she had paid her tuition she went to the room in the residence that she had chosen where
                        1   2   3
    she soon began unpacking her clothes.   22. 0 1 2 3 4
                4
23. The day was so warm and sunny that the entire class wished fervently that the lecture would take
                    1   2   3
    place outdoors.   23. 0 1 2 3 4
                4
24. Leonard Cohen who has recorded dozens of songs has also starred in the film *I Am a Hotel.* 24. 0 1 2 3 4
                    1   2   3   4
25. The road to Ayer's Cliff being coated with ice we proceeded slowly and cautiously.   25. 0 1 2 3 4
                            1   2   3   4

75

47. PUNCTUATION: THE COMMA

(Study P-1.)

The following sentences have commas that are either incorrect or absent. In the first column, write the word **after** which the comma that is there is wrong OR **after** which a comma is missing.
In the second column, select a **reason** for making your correction from the list below.
The sentence needs a comma because there is (are):

1. **two independent clauses joined by** *and, but, or, nor, for, yet*
2. **an introductory adverb clause**
3. **an introductory phrase (long prepositional, participial, infinitive, or absolute)**
4. **a series**
5. **an appositive**
6. **a nonrestrictive clause or phrase**

The comma that is there now is wrong because:

7. **There is no full clause after the conjunction.**
8. **The comma separates the subject from its verb.**
9. **The comma separates the verb from its complement.**
10. **There is a restrictive (or essential) clause.**

	Word	Reason
Example: When Frank and Joe looked around the stranger had vanished.	around	2
Example: The sun, shone brightly.	sun	8

1. There was much to do before her guests arrived for dinner but Betty did not know where to begin. 1. _____ ____

2. That it is indeed time for extremely serious commitment and concerted action on your part, is evident. 2. _____ ____

3. Having examined and reexamined the ancient manuscript the committee of scholars declared it genuine. 3. _____ ____

4. If Professor Fusty can convince the board that she is right, the curriculum will include Chaucer's major poems, and Shakespeare's major tragedies. 4. _____ ____

5. Michael has ambitious plans to finish his novel, start a play and work on his dissertation. 5. _____ ____

6. My brother who wants to be a pharmacist, attends York. 6. _____ ____

7. The character who is wearing the black hat and black cape, is the villain of the piece. 7. _____ ____

8. The bus having left an hour before we had no choice but to walk. 8. _____ ____

9. George and Robert thoroughly and painstakingly considered, what had to be done to defuse the bomb. 9. _____ ____

10. If ever there were the law on one side, and simple justice on the other, here is such a situation. 10. _____ ____

11. Clark Blaise, the author of *Lusts* is working on a new book. 11. _____ ____

12. Agatha began with the assumption that Max could not possibly have murdered Commodore Jenkins but she quickly came to doubt his innocence when she saw the footprints under the stairs.

12. _____ ___

13. Claiming that he was just offering good advice Ace frequently would tell me which card to play.

13. _____ ___

14. What gave Barbara the inspiration for her short story, was her mother's account of growing up on a farm.

14. _____ ___

15. Owen's hockey cards included such famous examples as Paul Henderson's winner against the Russians in 1982, and Wayne Gretzky breaking Gordie Howe's record.

15. _____ ___

16. The volume that was the most valuable in the library's rare book collection, was a First Folio edition of Shakespeare's plays.

16. _____ ___

17. A film enjoyed by millions of people throughout the world *Gone With the Wind* was first thought unlikely to be a commercial success.

17. _____ ___

18. With a triumphant cry and a finger pointing directly at Moriarty, Holmes demonstrated once again, that he was unequalled among the world's detectives.

18. _____ ___

19. Berger was appalled by how the Gursky family had made its fortune, but always believed in Solomon's greatness.

19. _____ ___

20. The criminal mind Jessica thought to herself, is even craftier than I had imagined.

20. _____ ___

48. PUNCTUATION: THE PERIOD, QUESTION MARK, AND EXCLAMATION POINT

(Study P-2 through P-4.)

Write **1** if the punctuation is **correct.**
Write **0** if it is **incorrect.**
(Use only one number in each blank.)

Example: Are we having fun yet[?]   <u> 1 </u>

1. You'd like that, wouldn't you[?]   1. _____

2. "Fire in number two engine!" the copilot shouted[!]   2. _____

3. The police officer calmly inquired if I had the slightest notion of just how fast I was backing up[?]   3. _____

4. Mr. Hall and Miss[.] James will chair the committee.   4. _____

5. I can't see you because I have to study all night for a math[.] quiz.   5. _____

6. Chickens, two goats, a pig, etc.[.], were wandering around the farmer's yard.   6. _____

7. Good afternoon, ma'am[.] May I present you with a free scrub brush?   7. _____

8. The homemaker asked[?], "May I know first, young man, what you're trying to sell?"   8. _____

9. His next question—wouldn't you know[?]—was, "What do you need, ma'am?"   9. _____

10. She said, "Is it too much to ask again, *'What* are you selling?'[?]"   10. _____

11. "What a magnificent view you have of the mountains[!]" said he.   11. _____

12. Who said, "If at first you don't succeed, [. . .] try again"?   12. _____

13. The man on the street corner told me that the special sale price of the watch would be $25[.] for just another ten minutes.   13. _____

14. HELP WANTED: Executive sec'y[.] with min. 4 yrs. exper.   14. _____

15. Pat, please type this memo[.] to the purchasing department.   15. _____

16. What? You lent that scoundrel Snively $10,000[?!]   16. _____

17. I asked her why, of all the men on campus, she had chosen him[?]   17. _____

18. Why did I do it? Because I loved her[.] Renée was the finest person I've ever known.   18. _____

19. Footloose and Fancy Free[.] [title of an essay]   19. _____

20. Would you please send me your reply by return mail[.]   20. _____

21. Your son ate my goldfish[?] Why didn't you just make him a hamburger?   21. _____

22. Charlie was an inspiring[(?)] date. He had me yawning all evening.   22. _____

23. "I can't [. . .] remember [. . .] her name," Sir Reginald gasped as the poison took effect.   23. _____

24. You must bring the following: (1[.]) your bat, (2[.]) your glove, and (3[.]) your baseball shoes.   24. _____

25. I heard the news on station C[.] B[.] M[.] T.   25. _____

49. PUNCTUATION: THE SEMICOLON

(Study P-5.)

Using the following list, write the number of the **reason** for the semicolon in each sentence. (Use only one number in each blank.)

1. **between independent clauses *not* joined by any conjunction or conjunctive adverb**
2. **between independent clauses joined by a conjunctive adverb (*however, therefore,* etc.)**
3. **between clauses joined by *and, but, or, nor, for,* or *yet* but having internal commas**
4. **to group items in a series**

Example: Everyone predicts the Jays will win the World Series; let's just wait and see. _____1_____

1. Parliament has now voted to spend more to protect wildlife; however, it may be already too late for many species. 1. _____

2. The farmers are using an improved fertilizer; thus their crop yields have increased. 2. _____

3. Still to come were Perry, a trained squirrel; Armand, an acrobat; and Marlene, a magician. 3. _____

4. "Negotiations," he said, "have collapsed; we will strike at noon." 4. _____

5. Read the questions carefully; answer each one as briefly as possible. 5. _____

6. Don first attended Vanier; then he went to McGill. 6. _____

7. Pam, who lives in the suburbs, drives her car to work each day; yet Clare, her next-door neighbor, takes the bus. 7. _____

8. She had paid her dues; therefore, she was eligible to vote. 8. _____

9. We stopped in Moncton, New Brunswick; Amherst, Nova Scotia; and Summerside, PEI. 9. _____

10. Cora was a fatalist; she believed that all events are predetermined. 10. _____

If **a semicolon** is needed within the brackets, insert it; then in the blank at the right, write the number (**1** to **4** from the list above) of the **reason** for that semicolon.
If **no semicolon** is needed within the brackets, write **0** in the blank.
(Use only one number in each blank.)

Example: I couldn't help you with your assignment[;] moreover, I wouldn't. _____2_____

1. She is going to the concert on Friday[ ] do you want her to get tickets for us? 1. _____

2. Shall I telephone to find out the time[ ] when the box office opens? 2. _____

3. Many of my college friends live in residences[ ] some still live at home. 3. _____

4. Louise read the help wanted ads[ ] and went to the campus Employment Center for weeks until, to her great relief, she found a summer job. 4. _____

5. She is very gifted[ ] two of her poems appear in an anthology. 5. _____

6. The surprises in Rodger's starting lineup were Garcia, the second baseman[ ] Hudler, the shortstop[ ] and Fitzgerald, the catcher. 6. _____

7. I was late for work[ ] because I had trouble finding a parking space. 7. _____

8. The subway was packed with commuters[ ] we were obliged to stand. 8. _____

9. Her boardinghouse burned down[ ] consequently, she had to find new lodgings. 9. _____

10. I tried several times to learn typing[ ] but, unfortunately, never succeeded. 10. _____

50. PUNCTUATION: THE SEMICOLON AND THE COMMA

(Study P-1 and P-5.)

Within the brackets, insert a comma, a semicolon, or nothing—whichever is **correct.** Then, in the blank at the right,

write **1** if you inserted **a comma** within the brackets;
write **2** if you inserted **a semicolon;**
write **0** if you inserted **nothing.**

(Use only one number in each blank.)

Example: The referee dropped the puck[;] the game began. _____2_____

1. The river remained calm[ ] still the guide refused to take us across.   1. _____

2. Tony signed the petition to maintain the green space downtown[ ] but several of his friends argued that the city needed investment.   2. _____

3. Dr. Jones[ ] who teaches geology[ ] graduated from UBC.   3. _____

4. The Dr. Jones[ ] who teaches geology[ ] graduated from UBC.   4. _____

5. I met the woman[ ] who is to be president of the new junior college.   5. _____

6. She likes working in Yellowknife, N.W.T.[ ] she hopes to remain there permanently.   6. _____

7. For the teenagers, the program was entertaining[ ] for the adults, it was boring.   7. _____

8. Read the article carefully[ ] then write an essay on the author's handling of the subject.   8. _____

9. I shall have to borrow a *Gazette*[ ] because I left my copy at home.   9. _____

10. The game being beyond our reach[ ] the coach told me to start warming up.   10. _____

11. We are going on a cruise around the bay on Sunday[ ] and we'd like you to come with us.   11. _____

12. If Amy decides to become a lawyer[ ] you can be sure she'll be a good one.   12. _____

13. I had worked in the library before[ ] therefore, I had no trouble getting a part-time job.   13. _____

14. Li-Young registered for an advanced biology course[ ] otherwise, she might not have been admitted to medical school.   14. _____

15. I would like[ ] however[ ] to pay the bridge toll for you. May I?   15. _____

16. The new rug has been delivered[ ] however, Terry is not pleased with its color.   16. _____

17. He began his speech again[ ] fire engines having drowned out his opening remarks.   17. _____

18. She somehow manages to find friends[ ] wherever she goes.   18. _____

19. Let me introduce the new officers: Phillip Whitaker, president[ ] Elaine Donatelli, secretary[ ] and Pierre Northrup, treasurer.   19. _____

20. The car did not need a new starter[ ] it needed only a tune-up.   20. _____

21. We had known the Floyd Archers[ ] ever since they moved here from New Brunswick.   21. _____

22. During the summer we visited friends in Ottawa[ ] Montreal[ ] and Toronto.   22. _____

23. The drama coach was a serene person[ ] not one to be worried by nervous amateurs.   23. _____

24. To turn them into professional performers was[ ] needless to say[ ] an impossible task.   24. _____

25. "No matter how hard I work," Frank said[ ] "I never seem to get an A."   25. _____

26. Call the security office[ ] if there seems to be any problem with the locks. 26. _____

27. She moved to Manitoba[ ] after she had sold her farm in Saskatchewan. 27. _____

28. Britain was the first Common Market country to react[ ] others quickly followed suit. 28. _____

29. The tanker ran aground in perfectly fair weather and calm seas[ ] the captain was fired. 29. _____

30. Because the weather was bad[ ] the picnic was moved indoors. 30. _____

51. PUNCTUATION: THE SEMICOLON AND THE COMMA

(Study P-1 and P-5.)

Within the brackets, insert a comma, a semicolon, or nothing—whichever is **correct.** Then, in the blank at the right,

write **1** if you inserted **a comma** within the brackets;
write **2** if you inserted **a semicolon;**
write **0** if you inserted **nothing.**

(Use only one number in each blank.)

Example: The television blared[;] the children sat motionless.   ___2___

1. Max's father launched into his usual diatribe about the younger generation[ ] the room quickly emptied.   1. _____

2. Into the cauldron the witches put a newt's eye[ ] a frog's toe[ ] and a pinch of henbane.   2. _____

3. "You're wondering why I called you here, aren't you?"[ ] the leader asked.   3. _____

4. The lead runner crested the hill[ ] and glanced back at the others struggling far behind.   4. _____

5. The score was tied[ ] the game would go into overtime.   5. _____

6. Blenchford studied all night[ ] but failed the test.   6. _____

7. Do you know[ ] Ms. Lane[ ] how we can get in touch with Superman?   7. _____

8. The first building on campus was an old[ ] dilapidated[ ] three-story structure.   8. _____

9. Time having run out[ ] I was obliged to hand in my test paper before I had finished.   9. _____

10. I spend too much time watching late shows on television[ ] I should be studying instead.   10. _____

11. All farmers[ ] who have had their crops destroyed by this year's drought[ ] will be compensated.   11. _____

12. Having written down the wrong page number[ ] I read the wrong chapter.   12. _____

13. She had been in the hospital[ ] she had missed three weeks of classes.   13. _____

14. During his first three years of college[ ] he attended three different institutions.   14. _____

15. Having learned that the meeting had been postponed[ ] John went back to the library.   15. _____

16. Poised and completely at ease[ ] the student-body president greeted the incoming freshmen.   16. _____

17. "The answer is here somewhere," Holmes said[ ] "and I'm sure we can find it."   17. _____

18. We stood shivering[ ] the sun having gone behind the clouds.   18. _____

19. Ms. Vane, the principal, waited[ ] until the students in the assembly hall were quiet.   19. _____

20. The mayor adjusted his tie, smiled, and coughed[ ] then he said he was glad that the question had
been asked.   20. _____

21. Having my arm in a cast bothered me[ ] but the doctor insisted that a cast was necessary.   21. _____

22. In a nearby park, children were shouting happily[ ] their noise did not disturb us.   22. _____

23. Professor Curtis has left the campus[ ] however, she may be reached by telephone.   23. _____

24. This certainly is the best of all possible worlds[ ] don't you think?   24. _____

25. They were married[ ] while they were still medical students at McMaster.   25. _____

26. After they graduated, they packed their belongings[ ] and moved to a small town in Ontario. 26. _____

27. Amy was aware as she raced down the hill[ ] that this would be her last chance ever to win a medal in the downhill. 27. _____

28. He teaches freshman English[ ] Speech II[ ] and a literature course. 28. _____

29. Your behavior is unacceptable, Mr. Flashman[ ] we shall have to expel you. 29. _____

30. Our representatives included Will Leeds, a member of the Rotary Club[ ] Augusta Allcott, a banker[ ] and Bill Rogers, president of the Chamber of Commerce. 30. _____

31. The Prime Minister ordered his aides to start an inquiry into the oil spill[ ] and to report back to him within the week. 31. _____

32. She expects to graduate in June[ ] then she will spend the summer in Europe. 32. _____

33. He followed the trail to the summit[ ] later, he found the entrance to the mine. 33. _____

34. "She is," the coach said, "an excellent golfer[ ] and a fine student." 34. _____

35. Without seeing where I made my mistakes on my essay[ ] I simply can't hope to do better next time. 35. _____

36. Peter lives in Yellowknife[ ] Howard, in Timmons. 36. _____

37. The teacher asked[ ] that everyone be quiet. 37. _____

38. His adviser's signature being required[ ] Fred went to the administration building. 38. _____

39. Failing to make the right turn on the highway[ ] caused us to arrive two hours late. 39. _____

40. Fighting his way through a host of tacklers[ ] he scored a touchdown. 40. _____

41. My uncle's barn[ ] not his house[ ] had burned to the ground. 41. _____

42. As Mark Twain said, the rain will stop[ ] it usually does. 42. _____

43. Upon graduating from college[ ] he went into the service. 43. _____

44. Vacation time is almost over[ ] there are only four days left. 44. _____

45. "When we go to British Columbia[ ] I would like to stay for a week in Victoria," she said. 45. _____

46. After attending his chemistry and psychology classes[ ] Leslie sat down to write a letter. 46. _____

47. We didn't go to the theater[ ] for we had heard that no good seats were left. 47. _____

48. Frank was angry with Gail[ ] for having broken her promise to him to be prompt. 48. _____

49. He asked you to help him with his biology[ ] didn't he? 49. _____

50. They suspected it might be found[ ] if someone were to look through the gym lockers. 50. _____

51. We decided not to watch the late movie[ ] all of us wanting to get a good night's sleep. 51. _____

52. The Grey Cup hadn't yet begun[ ] however, he had equipped himself with a new transistor radio. 52. _____

53. I couldn't remember having seen her as radiantly happy[ ] as she now was. 53. _____

54. No, I cannot go to the game[ ] I have a term paper to finish. 54. _____

55. "I don't know the answer[ ] in fact, I didn't hear your question," she said indifferently. 55. _____

56. Victor[ ] on the other hand[ ] played the best game of his career. 56. _____

57. Genevieve laughed hysterically[ ] Marie, on the other hand, was very serious. 57. _____

58. "There will be no rain today[ ]" she insisted. "The weather forecaster says so." 58. _____

59. The stores were crowded[ ] the Christmas rush having started. 59. _____

60. Although he majored in math in college[ ] he has trouble dividing a lunch check. 60. _____

52. PUNCTUATION: THE APOSTROPHE

(Study P-6.)

In the first column, write the number of the **correct** choice (**1** or **2**).
In the second column, write the number (**3** to **6**, from the list below) of the **reason** for your choice. (If your choice has **no apostrophe**, write nothing in the second column.)

3. singular possessive   5. contraction
4. plural possessive   6. plural of letter, number, symbol, word used as word

	Word Choice	Reason for Choice
Example: The day is (1)our's (2)ours.	2	
1. I (1)*didn't* (2)*did'nt* have enough money with me to pay the taxi.	1. ___ ___	
2. The (1)*Smith's* (2)*Smiths* have invited us to their daughter's wedding.	2. ___ ___	
3. The (1)*James'* (2)*Jameses* are moving to Saskatoon.	3. ___ ___	
4. My (1)*brother-in-law's* (2)*brother's-in-law* wife is a pediatrician.	4. ___ ___	
5. The (1)*Russo's* (2)*Russos* have a two-year-old son.	5. ___ ___	
6. Our family cat was delighted with (1)*its* (2)*it's* very own scratching post.	6. ___ ___	
7. The principal demanded, "(1)*Who's* (2)*Whose* responsible for this vandalism?"	7. ___ ___	
8. The two (1)*girl's* (2)*girls'* talent was quite evident to everyone.	8. ___ ___	
9. We will be at the (1)*Lopez's* (2)*Lopezes'* home until midnight.	9. ___ ___	
10. It will be a two-(1)*day's* (2)*days'* drive to the ocean.	10. ___ ___	
11. He went on a three (1)*weeks'* (2)*week's* vacation trip to Cuba.	11. ___ ___	
12. To get ahead, she planned to win her (1)*bosses* (2)*boss's* favor.	12. ___ ___	
13. After the long absence, they fell into (1)*each others'* (2)*each other's* arms.	13. ___ ___	
14. From its friendly greeting, it was evident that the dog was (1)*her's* (2)*hers.*	14. ___ ___	
15. Geraldine uses too many (1)*ands* (2)*and's* in most of her speeches.	15. ___ ___	
16. His (1)*O's* (2)*Os* have a solid black center; his printer needs to be cleaned.	16. ___ ___	
17. (1)*Wer'ent* (2)*Weren't* you surprised to see him so soon?	17. ___ ___	
18. Is this Dan and Betty's canoe, or is it (1)*ours* (2)*our's*?	18. ___ ___	
19. Georgiana insisted, "I (1)*have'nt* (2)*haven't* seen Sandy for weeks."	19. ___ ___	
20. He bought fifty (1)*cents* (2)*cents'* worth of popcorn.	20. ___ ___	
21. The back alley was known to be a (1)*thieve's* (2)*thieves'* hangout.	21. ___ ___	
22. There were far too many (1)*but's* (2)*buts* in his praise of my essay.	22. ___ ___	
23. He noticed that the (1)*children's* (2)*childrens'* shoes were caked with mud.	23. ___ ___	
24. "Your (1)*times* (2)*time's* up," announced the testing officer.	24. ___ ___	
25. The (1)*coal miner's* (2)*coal miners'* union went on strike for higher wages.	25. ___ ___	

53. PUNCTUATION: THE APOSTROPHE

(Study P-6.)

For each bracketed apostrophe,

write **1** if it is **correct;**
write **0** if it is **incorrect.**

(Use the first column for the first apostrophe in each sentence; use the second column for the second apostrophe.)

Example: *Who*[']*s* on first? Where's *todays*['] lineup?   1   0

1. This is no one *else*[']*s* fault but *your*[']*s,* I'm sorry to say.   1. _____ _____

2. Mrs. *Leclerc*[']*s* invitation to the *William*[']*s* must have gone astray.   2. _____ _____

3. He *would*[']*nt* know that after only two *day*[']*s* employment.   3. _____ _____

4. *Wer*[']*en't* they fortunate that the damaged car wasn't *their*[']*s*?   4. _____ _____

5. *It*[']*s* a pity that the one bad cabin would be *their*[']*s.*   5. _____ _____

6. *We*[']*re* expecting the *Wagner*[']*s* to meet us in Edmonton next summer.   6. _____ _____

7. *"Where*[']*s* your driver's license?"' was the *officer*[']*s* first question.   7. _____ _____

8. "What Mary *does*[']*nt* know *won*[']*t* worry her," he said.   8. _____ _____

9. The two sisters had agreed that *they*[']*d* not wear each *others*['] clothes.   9. _____ _____

10. *She*[']*s* the sort of person who won't listen to *anybody*[']*s* opinion but her own.   10. _____ _____

11. The *childrens*['] balloons were distributed at my little *sister*[']*s* birthday party yesterday afternoon.   11. _____ _____

12. *He*[']*s* hoping to get two *hours*['] work each day in the school cafeteria.   12. _____ _____

13. The idea of starting a scholarship fund was not *our*[']*s; * it was *Lois*[']*s.*   13. _____ _____

14. There are three *i*[']*s* in the word *optimistic;* there are two *r*[']*s* in the word *embarrass.*   14. _____ _____

15. The computer printout consisted of a series of *1*[']*s* and *0*[']*s.*   15. _____ _____

16. I sent two dozen red *roses*['] to the members of the *Mothers*['] Club.   16. _____ _____

17. I really *did*[']*nt* expect to see all of the *drivers*['] finish the race.   17. _____ _____

18. Is it possible that you *hav*[']*ent* heard about the fire at the *Jone*[']*s* house?   18. _____ _____

19. Tabby, usually the *mices*['] tormentor, *was*[']*nt* interested in chasing them any longer.   19. _____ _____

20. I'm sure that, if *he*[']*s* physically able, *he*[']*ll* play in next Saturday's football game.   20. _____ _____

21. The responsibility for notifying club members is *her*[']*s,* not *our*[']*s.*   21. _____ _____

22. *Can*[']*t* I persuade you that *you*[']*re* now financially able to own your own car?   22. _____ _____

23. I sent word to the *Cohens*['] that *we*[']*d* see them on Sunday.   23. _____ _____

24. The address on the envelope was not *our*[']*s;* it was the *Burgesses*['].   24. _____ _____

25. My *mother-in-law*[']*s* books are aimed at the *children*[']*s* market.   25. _____ _____

54. PUNCTUATION: THE APOSTROPHE

(Study P-6.)

In the paragraph below, every word ending in *s* has a number beneath it. Only **eleven** of these words need apostrophes. In each corresponding blank at the right,

write **1** if the word should end in **'s;**
write **2** if the word should end in **s';**
write **0** if the word needs **no apostrophe.**

Example: We took showers after the game.   40. __0__
                                          40

A junior hockey players fondest dreams concern being drafted by the professionals. If a teams star   1. _____
               1   2   3   4
averages three or four points a game or makes an all-star team, that youngsters phone rings   2. _____
        5   6   7   8   9
constantly, and his mail carriers bag overflows with good wishes from admirers. Yet very often,   3. _____
            10   11   12   13   14
this young players hopes are falsely aroused by illusions of riches that turn out to be no better than   4. _____
15   16   17   18   19
an ordinary persons salary. The medias descriptions of exciting arenas overflowing with lively,   5. _____
            20   21   22   23

6. _____

7. _____

8. _____

9. _____

10. _____

11. _____

12. _____

13. _____

14. _____

15. _____

16. _____

17. _____

18. _____

19. _____

20. _____

21. _____

22. _____

23. _____

eager members   of the opposite sex can stimulate a boys   imagination to the point where no reality can
      24   25

match what the minds eye envisions. The young persons disappointment becomes all the keener
           26   27   28   29

when he learns that salary offers from the teams that he might sign with are too low for the
         30   31   32

dreams fulfillment.
     33

24. _____

25. _____

26. _____

27. _____

28. _____

29. _____

30. _____

31. _____

32. _____

33. _____

55. PUNCTUATION: ITALICS

(Study P-7.)

Write the number of the **reason** for each use of italics:

1. **title of book, magazine, or newspaper**
2. **title of musical production, play, film, or TV show**
3. **name of ship, aircraft, or spacecraft**
4. **title of painting or sculpture**
5. **foreign word not yet anglicized**
6. **word, letter, figure, or symbol referred to as such**
7. **emphasis**

Example: I read nothing but *TV Guide*.   __1__

1. The *Titanic* was thought to be an unsinkable ship.   1. _____
2. *The Wizard of Oz* seems to be shown on television every Easter.   2. _____
3. For many years the Manchester *Guardian* has been a leading newspaper in England.   3. _____
4. Much comment resulted from a recent article in *Maclean's* magazine.   4. _____
5. Directions on the test indicated that all questions were to be answered with *1*'s or *2*'s.   5. _____
6. A mnemonic device for helping a student to spell the word *principal* is the expression "The *principal* is your *pal*."   6. _____
7. Susan learned to spell the word *villain* by thinking of a *villa in* Italy.   7. _____
8. She subscribes to *Saturday Night*, *MTL*, and *Time* magazines.   8. _____
9. Shakespeare's *Hamlet* is to be the next production of the Little Theater group.   9. _____
10. An article had been written recently about the *Anik II* satellite.   10. _____
11. Tom Wolfe's book about the space program is called *The Right Stuff*.   11. _____
12. How many *s*'s and *a*'s are there in *Saskatchewan*?   12. _____
13. Many sports lovers consider *Sports Illustrated* one of their favorite magazines.   13. _____
14. Canadians pronounce *vase* either *vās* or *väz*.   14. _____
15. Carol Goar of the *Toronto Star* has won prizes for her commentary on politics.   15. _____
16. "Even though you are very busy, you *must* get more rest," said the doctor.   16. _____
17. Aboard the *Enterprise*, the captain made plans to return to the planet Zircon to rescue Mr. Spock.   17. _____
18. He has a leading role in the opera *Pagliacci*, hasn't he?   18. _____
19. She went to Italy aboard the luxury liner *Michelangelo*.   19. _____
20. The first Canadian in space was Marc Garneau.   20. _____
21. Her printed *R*'s and *B*'s closely resemble each other.   21. _____
22. Although he never held office, Lopez was the *de facto* ruler of his country.   22. _____
23. Some people spell and pronounce the words *athlete* and *athletics* as if there were an *e* after the *th* in each word.   23. _____
24. Dustin Hoffman's portrayal of an autistic savant in *The Rain Man* won him his second Oscar.   24. _____
25. The original meaning of the word *mad* was "disordered in mind" or "insane."   25. _____

In each sentence there is **one** word or set of words that should be **italicized.** Underline these words, and write in the blank the number (**1** to **7**, from the list on page 88) of the **reason** for the italics.

Example: He was on the cover of <u>Saturday Night</u>.   <u> 1 </u>

1. "The Shadow" is a poem in Irving Layton's collection The Pole-Vaulter.   1. _____

2. Deciding to come home by ship, we made reservations on the Queen Elizabeth II.   2. _____

3. Geraldine went downtown to buy copies of Esquire, Chatelaine, and Vista.   3. _____

4. "Just watch me," said Trudeau, and we did.   4. _____

5. Indians was a prize-winning play in 1989.   5. _____

6. The Montreal Gazette must have weighed five pounds last Saturday.   6. _____

7. The World at War was a highly praised television documentary of the 1980s.   7. _____

8. Findley's The Telling of Lies has always been one of Edward's favorite books.   8. _____

9. Among the magazines lying on the table was a copy of Canadian Business.   9. _____

10. Footprints on the Moon, Maureen Hutner's play about mothers and daughters, was highly praised.   10. _____

11. When I try to pronounce the word statistics, I always stumble over it.   11. _____

12. She seems unaware of the difference between the words accept and except.   12. _____

13. "There is no such word as alright," said Miss Williams, frowning as she wrote it on the chalkboard.   13. _____

14. Picasso's Guernica depicts the horrors of war.   14. _____

15. The Thinker is a statue that many people admire.   15. _____

16. Lawrence of Arabia is considered an outstanding motion picture of the 1960s.   16. _____

17. You'll enjoy reading "Winter at Home" in the book Three Seasons of Sky.   17. _____

18. The British spelling of the word jail is g-a-o-l.   18. _____

19. "What Is College For?" is an essay by Max McConn in Modern English Readings.   19. _____

20. Michelangelo's Last Judgment shows "the omnipotence of his artistic ability."   20. _____

21. The source of the above quotation is the Canadian Encyclopedia.   21. _____

22. The fourth opera in this winter's series is Verdi's Don Carlo.   22. _____

23. Her argument was ad hominem.   23. _____

24. Perry won the spelling bee's award for creative expression with his rendition of antidisestablishmentarianism.   24. _____

25. The instructor said that Sam's 7's and his 4's look very much alike.   25. _____

56. PUNCTUATION: QUOTATION MARKS

(Study P-8.)

Insert **quotation marks** (double or single, as needed) at the proper places in each sentence. Then, in the blank at the right, write the number (**1** to **12** from the list below) of the **reason** for the quotation marks:

1. **direct quotation**
2. **title of chapter**
3. **title of magazine article**
4. **title of short story**
5. **title of essay**
6. **title of poem**
7. **title of song**
8. **title of one-act play**
9. **title of lecture**
10. **title of newspaper article or editorial**
11. **definition**
12. **nickname**

Example: *Expedite* means "to facilitate or advance."   ___11___

1. The article about silk, The Queen of Textiles, appeared in *National Geographic* magazine in January 1984.   1. _____

2. Murder in the Rain Forest, which appeared in *Vanity Fair* magazine, told of the death of a courageous Brazilian environmentalist.   2. _____

3. W. C. Fields' dying words were I'd rather be in Philadelphia.   3. _____

4. The poem The Swing was written by Robert Louis Stevenson.   4. _____

5. I am confident, said the candidate, that I will win.   5. _____

6. Use of the Dictionary is a chapter in the textbook *Correct Writing*.   6. _____

7. In the magazine *Canadian Geographic,* John Robbins describes the Arctic in an article titled A Fragile Beauty.   7. _____

8. The word *cavalier* was originally defined as a man on a horse.   8. _____

9. Gordon Red Johnson stood up to address the members of the football team.   9. _____

10. Silent Night is a song heard frequently during the Christmas season.   10. _____

11. One of my favorite short stories is Timothy Findley's Stones.   11. _____

12. Did the professor give the lecture Abnormal Behavior last semester?   12. _____

13. The World Is Too Much with Us is a poem by William Wordsworth.   13. _____

14. The Younger Generation is an article that appeared in *Time* magazine.   14. _____

15. An article that appeared in the *Ottawa Citizen* is Can We Save the Earth?   15. _____

16. Bacon's essay, Of Fortune, comments sadly on the brevity of human friendship.   16. _____

17. The Love Song of J. Alfred Prufrock is a poem by T. S. Eliot.   17. _____

18. Sunrise is a one-act play by Tom Scott.   18. _____

19. The concluding song of the evening was Auld Lang Syne.   19. _____

20. We read a poem by Edna St. Vincent Millay entitled Love Is Not All.   20. _____

21. A Polluted River is the title of an editorial in the *Hamilton Spectator*.   21. _____

22. Otis took hitting lessons from Harry The Hat Walker.   22. _____

23. We read The Keys to Dreamland, an essay by Northrop Frye.   23. _____

24. She enjoyed Roger Kaufmann's short story, The Nearness of You.   24. _____

25. *Discography* means a comprehensive list of recordings made by a particular performer or of a particular composer's work.   25. _____

57. PUNCTUATION: QUOTATION MARKS

(Study P-8.)

Write **1** if the punctuation in brackets is **correct.**
Write **0** if it is **incorrect.**
(Use only one number in each blank.)

Example: "Want to play ball, Scarecrow[?]" the Wicked Witch wondered, a ball of fire in her hand.	_1_
1. The late arrivals asked[, "]When did the party end?"	1. _____
2. When the job was finished, the worker asked, "How do you like it[?"]	2. _____
3. In the first semester, we read Joyce's "The Dead[".]	3. _____
4. "Where are you presently employed?[",] the interviewer asked.	4. _____
5. "Whenever I see Joan," said Ellen[, "]she always asks for you."	5. _____
6. Who was it who mused "Where are the snows of yesteryear["?]	6. _____
7. Dr. Nelson, my math teacher, asked, "Who wants me to repeat the explanation[?"]	7. _____
8. "You're out of your mind![",] exclaimed Lydia, slamming down her books.	8. _____
9. "Write when you can[,"] Mother said as I left for the airport.	9. _____
10. *To sympathize* means ["]to share in suffering or grief[."]	10. _____
11. "Ask not what your country can do for you[;"] ask what you can do for your country."	11. _____
12. The bus driver said, "To the east is the courthouse.["] ["]Buses stop there every half hour."	12. _____
13. "Do you remember Father's saying, 'Never give up['?"] she asked.	13. _____
14. She began reciting the opening lines of Elizabeth Barrett Browning's sonnet "How do I love thee? Let me count the ways[."]	14. _____
15. Margaret Atwood's poem ["]You Are Happy["] is one of her best.	15. _____
16. ["]The Mousetrap["] is the longest-running play in British theater.	16. _____
17. She said, "Don't you get tired of hearing everyone sing 'Don't Worry, Be Happy[?' "]	17. _____
18. "Shall I read aloud Layton's poem 'Song for Naomi['?"] he asked.	18. _____
19. Have you read Adrienne Rich's poem "Necessities of Life[?"]	19. _____
20. When she saw his new Corvette, she exclaimed, "What a beautiful car[!"]	20. _____
21. The noun *neurotic* is defined as "an emotionally unstable individual[".]	21. _____
22. "I'm going to the newsstand," he said[; "]for a copy of *Toronto Life.*"	22. _____
23. "Do you believe in fairies[?"] Peter Pan asks the children.	23. _____
24. How maddening of her to reply calmly, "You're so right["!]	24. _____
25. "Come as soon as you can," said Mother to the plumber[. "]The basement is already flooded."	25. _____
26. I heard Andy say, "Mike asked, 'Who are the new neighbors down the street['?"]	26. _____
27. "The Lottery[,"] a short story by Shirley Jackson, was discussed in Janet's English class.	27. _____
28. Did you read Krutch's article, "Is the Common Man Too Common?["?]	28. _____

92

29. "Was the treaty signed in 1763[?"] the professor asked, "or in 1764?" 29. _____

30. The mayor said, "I guarantee that urban renewal will move forward rapidly[;"] however, I don't believe him. 30. _____

58. PUNCTUATION: ITALICS AND QUOTATION MARKS

(Study P-7 and P-8.)

Write the number of the **correct** choice.

Example: A revival of Cole Porter's play (1)*Anything Goes* (2)"Anything Goes" played at the Shaw Festival.   1. ___1___

1. (1)"Cats," (2)*Cats,* which toured Canada, is based on the work of T. S. Eliot.   1. _____

2. An editorial titled (1)*Make the Subway Safe* (2)"Make the Subway Safe" appeared in the *Toronto Sun.*   2. _____

3. (1)"London Bridge" (2)*London Bridge* is a popular nursery rhyme.   3. _____

4. Paul Kennedy's book (1)*The Rise and Fall of the Great Powers* (2)"The Rise and Fall of the Great Powers" discusses how nations become politically and militarily dominant.   4. _____

5. The title of the *Maclean's* article is (1)*Faculty Survival* (2)"Faculty Survival."   5. _____

6. The closing song around the campfire was (1)"Good Night, Ladies." (2)*Good Night, Ladies.*   6. _____

7. (1)*A Haunted House* (2)"A Haunted House" is a short story by Virginia Woolf.   7. _____

8. The tone of Al Purdy's poem (1)*Transient* (2)"Transient" appealed to her.   8. _____

9. Helene received (1)*A's* (2)"A's" in three of her classes this fall.   9. _____

10. She used too many (1)*and's* (2)"and's" in her introductory speech.   10. _____

11. (1)*Science and Religion* (2)"Science and Religion" is an essay by Albert Einstein.   11. _____

12. He has purchased tickets for the opera (1)"Faust." (2)*Faust.*   12. _____

13. A careless printer had misspelled the word (1)*psychology.* (2)"psychology."   13. _____

14. Dr. Baylor spent an entire class on Leonard Cohen's poem (1)"Saint Catherine Street." (2)*Saint Catherine Street.*   14. _____

15. His favorite newspaper has always been the (1)*Times.* (2)"Times."   15. _____

16. (1)"Our Town" (2)*Our Town* is a play by Thornton Wilder.   16. _____

17. The word *altogether* means (1)"wholly" or "thoroughly." (2)*wholly* or *thoroughly.*   17. _____

18. (1)*What Women Want* (2)"What Women Want" is an essay by Margaret Mead.   18. _____

19. Dave Thompson's short story (1)*Help Me—I Love You* (2)"Help Me—I Love You" amused her.   19. _____

20. The Players' Guild will produce Marlowe's (1)*Dr. Faustus* (2)"Dr. Faustus" next month.   20. _____

21. Herbert Kim's essay (1)*The Design of a PASCAL Compiler* (2)"The Design of a PASCAL Compiler" appeared in the May 1987 edition of *The Journal of Computer Languages.*   21. _____

22. (1)*Perspectives* (2)"Perspectives" is the title of the textbook we were to use.   22. _____

23. I purchased a copy of Earl Birney's (1)"Collected Poems." (2)*Collected Poems.*   23. _____

24. Our film class saw Truffaut's (1)*Shoot the Piano Player* (2)"Shoot the Piano Player" last week. 24. _____

25. She read (1)*Dover Beach,* (2)"Dover Beach," a poem by Matthew Arnold.   25. _____

26. (1)*Pygmalion* (2)"Pygmalion" is a play by George Bernard Shaw. 26. _____

27. You fail to distinguish between the words (1)*range* and *vary.* (2)"range" and "vary." 27. _____

28. I read a poem by Yeats titled (1)"The Cat and the Moon." (2)*The Cat and the Moon.* 28. _____

29. She rarely purchases copies of (1)*Reader's Digest.* (2)"Reader's Digest." 29. _____

30. (1)*Fortune My Foe* (2)"Fortune My Foe" is a play by Robertson Davies. 30. _____

59. PUNCTUATION: THE COLON, THE DASH, PARENTHESES, AND BRACKETS

(Study P-9 through P-12.)

The Colon

Write **1** if the colon in brackets is used **correctly**.
Write **0** if it is used **incorrectly**.

Example: We invited: Larry, Moe, and Curly.	0
1. Casey's first question was[:] Can anybody here play this game?	1. _____
2. The coach signaled the strategy[:] we would lift the goaltender in the last minute.	2. _____
3. Dear Sir[:] My six years' experience as a legal secretary qualifies me for the position advertised.	3. _____
4. Dear "Stretch"[:] The whole group—all eight of us—plan to spend the weekend with you.	4. _____
5. Laura's shopping list included these items: truffles, caviar, champagne, and a dozen hot dogs.	5. _____
6. The carpenter brought his[:] saw, hammer, square, measuring tape, and nails.	6. _____
7. Children usually enjoy[:] candy, ice cream, and cookies.	7. _____
8. She began her letter to Tom with these words[:] "You stupid fool!"	8. _____
9. I knew that her plane left on Tuesday at approximately 3[:]30 P.M.	9. _____
10. The dean demanded that[:] the coaches, the players, and the training staff meet with him immediately.	10. _____
11. Tonight's winning numbers are[:] 169, 534, and 086.	11. _____
12. She was warned that the project would require one thing[:] perseverance.	12. _____

The Dash, Parentheses, and Brackets

Set off the boldface words by inserting the **correct** punctuation. Then write the number of the punctuation you inserted:

1. dash(es)   2. parentheses   3. brackets

Example: Sheila Finestone (**Lib., Mt. Royal**) voted against the bill on first reading.	2
1. It's raining too hard to go to school today **just look out the window.**	1. _____
2. Holmes had deduced **who knew how?** that the man had been born on a moving train during the rainy season. [*Punctuate to indicate a sharp interruption.*]	2. _____
3. He will be considered for **this is between you and me, of course** one of the three vice-presidencies in the firm. [*Punctuate to indicate merely incidental comment.*]	3. _____
4. I simply told her **and I'm glad I did!** that I would never set foot in her house again. [*Punctuate to indicate merely incidental comment.*]	4. _____
5. Within the last year, I have received three **or was it four?** letters from her. [*Punctuate to indicate merely incidental comment.*]	5. _____

6. At Banff National Park we watched the feeding of the tourists *from a safe distance, you can be sure.* [*Punctuate to achieve a dramatic effect.*]   6. _____

7. Her essay was entitled "The Canadian Medical System and It's *sic* Problems."   7. _____

8. The rules for using parentheses *see page 7* are not difficult to master.   8. _____

9. Only one thing stood in the way of his buying the yellow Cadillac *money.*   9. _____

10. The statement read: "Enclosed you will find one hundred dollars *$100* to cover damages."   10. _____

11. ELECTRA *with a cry:* Oh! You liar!   11. _____

12. *Eat, drink, and be merry* gosh, I can hardly wait for study week.   12. _____

13. The essay begins: "For more than a hundred years *from 1337 until 1453* the British and French fought a pointless war." [*Punctuate to show that the boldface expression is inserted editorially.*]   13. _____

14. The concert begins at *by the way, when does the concert begin?*   14. _____

15. Getting to work at eight o'clock every morning *I don't have to remind you how much I dislike getting up early* seemed almost more than I cared to undertake. [*Punctuate to indicate merely incidental comment.*]   15. _____

16. She said, "Two of my friends *one has really serious emotional problems* need psychiatric help." [*Punctuate to achieve a dramatic effect.*]   16. _____

17. Campbell's work on Juvenal *see References* is an excellent place to start.   17. _____

18. Julius was born in 1900 *?* and came west as a young boy.   18. _____

19. Gerri had only one aim in life *to follow in her mother's footsteps in the medical profession.*   19. _____

20. I'll play *what can I play?*   20. _____

21. Churchill told a cheering House of Commons, "You *Hitler* do your worst, and we will do our best." [*Punctuate to show that the boldface expression is inserted editorially.*]   21. _____

22. I would never consider selling my grandmother's earrings *unless you increase your offer.*   22. _____

23. This should be the third out *oh no, the ball bounces off Smith's helmet!*   23. _____

24. BATMAN *in a shocked tone:* He's taken my what?   24. _____

25. To start the program, simply **1** insert the disk in drive A, and **2** turn on the power switch.   25. _____

60. PUNCTUATION: THE HYPHEN

(Study P-13.)

Write **1** if the use or omission of a hyphen is **correct.**
Write **0** if it is **incorrect.**

Example: *Seventy six* trombones led the big parade. ⎯⎯⎯0⎯⎯⎯

1. Mr. Pollard's major research interest was **seventeenth-century** French history. 1. _____
2. Dana made a **semi-serious** effort to pick up the check. 2. _____
3. Debbie certainly is a good old-fashioned **Canadian** girl. 3. _____
4. "I **c-c-can't** breathe," the child panted. 4. _____
5. The **six-year-old** boy climbed onto the speaker's platform and sat down. 5. _____
6. She rented a **two room** apartment on the other side of town. 6. _____
7. The speaker was **well known** to everyone connected with administration. 7. _____
8. A **well-known** scientist will conduct a seminar during summer session. 8. _____
9. The Blue Jays averaged over **fifty-thousand** spectators a game when the Skydome opened. 9. _____
10. The contractor expects to build many **five-** and **six-room** houses this year. 10. _____
11. The club president sent a **skillfully-worded** statement to the city editor. 11. _____
12. We sent Joanne a new **five dollar** bill for her birthday. 12. _____
13. I sent in my subscription to a new **bi-monthly** magazine. 13. _____
14. **Semi-infinite** space, the television producer explained, is where the captain and crew will find the semifinal frontier. 14. _____
15. Susan had found her **mother-in-law** to be a very helpful person with the children. 15. _____
16. At last her dream of an **up to date** kitchen was coming true. 16. _____
17. He made every effort to **recover** the missing gems. 17. _____
18. She had bought fabric with which to **re-cover** her husband's favorite chair. 18. _____
19. Yossarian had another long chat with **excorporal** Wintergreen. 19. _____
20. At **eighty-two,** Aunt Mary is as active as ever. 20. _____
21. Charles will run in the **hundred yard** dash next Saturday. 21. _____
22. "The children are not to have any more **c-a-n-d-y,**" said Mother. 22. _____
23. After he graduated from college, he became manager of the **student-owned** bookstore. 23. _____
24. The idea of a **forty hour** week appealed to the workers. 24. _____
25. A world record had been set in the **120 yard** high hurdles. 25. _____
26. Baird played **semi-professional** hockey before going into the NHL. 26. _____
27. Customers began avoiding the **hot-tempered** clerk in the shoe department. 27. _____
28. His friends tried to restore Al's **self-confidence.** 28. _____
29. Congratulations, Myrtle—you've won a sensational, fantastic, **brand new** gum irrigator! 29. _____
30. Myrtle's gum irrigator was **brand new.** 30. _____

61. PUNCTUATION: REVIEW

(Study P.)

Write **1** for each statement that is **true**.
Write **0** for each that is **false**.

Example: A *period* is used at the end of a declarative sentence.	__1__
1. *Single quotation marks* are used to enclose a quotation within a quotation.	1. _____
2. An *apostrophe* is used to indicate the possessive case of personal pronouns.	2. _____
3. The *question mark* is always placed *inside* closing quotation marks.	3. _____
4. A *dash* may be indicated by the use of two hyphens on the typewriter.	4. _____
5. A *dash* is used before the author's name following a direct quotation.	5. _____
6. *Parentheses* are used to enclose editorial remarks in a direct quotation.	6. _____
7. *No commas* are used to set off a restrictive adjective clause.	7. _____
8. A *semicolon* is used to set off an absolute phrase from the rest of the sentence.	8. _____
9. The use of *brackets* around the word *sic* indicates an error occurring in quoted material.	9. _____
10. Mild interjections should be followed by an *exclamation point;* strong ones, by a *comma.*	10. _____
11. An indirect question is followed by a *period.*	11. _____
12. A *semicolon* is used after the expression *Dear Sir.*	12. _____
13. The title of a magazine article should be underlined to designate the use of *italics.*	13. _____
14. *Ms.* takes a period but *Miss* does not.	14. _____
15. The title of a newspaper is enclosed in *double quotation marks.*	15. _____
16. *Mr. Jone's, Mr. Jones',* and *Mr. Jones's* are all acceptable *possessive* forms of *Mr. Jones.*	16. _____
17. The title at the head of a composition should be enclosed in *double quotation marks.*	17. _____
18. *No apostrophe* is needed in the following greeting: "Merry Christmas from the Palmers."	18. _____
19. The *possessive* of *somebody else* is *somebody's else.*	19. _____
20. The *possessive* of *mother-in-law* is *mother's-in-law.*	20. _____
21. A *semicolon* is used between two independent clauses joined by *and* if one or both clauses contain internal commas.	21. _____
22. A quotation consisting of several sentences takes *double quotation marks* at the beginning of the first sentence and at the end of the last sentence.	22. _____
23. A quotation consisting of several paragraphs takes *double quotation marks* at the beginning and end of each paragraph.	23. _____
24. The *plurals* of words, letters, or numbers (referred to as such) are formed by the addition of *'s* to the singular form.	24. _____
25. The word *the* is *italicized* in the name of a newspaper or a magazine.	25. _____
26. A polite request in the form of a question is followed by a *period.*	26. _____
27. *Single quotation marks* may be substituted for double quotation marks around any quoted passage.	27. _____

28. The **comma** is always placed *outside* closing quotation marks.   28. _____

29. The **colon** and **semicolon** are always placed *inside* quotation marks.   29. _____

30. A **comma** is always used to separate the two parts of a compound predicate.   30. _____

31. The expression *such as* is always followed by a **comma.**   31. _____

32. The nonsentence is a legitimate unit of expression and may be followed by a **period.**   32. _____

33. When a declarative sentence is followed by a confirmatory question, a **comma** is used between them.   33. _____

34. **Parentheses** are used around words that are to be deleted from a manuscript.   34. _____

35. A **comma** is used between two independent clauses not joined by a coordinating conjunction.   35. _____

36. A **semicolon** is used after the salutation of a business letter.   36. _____

37. The subject of a sentence should be separated from the predicate by use of a **comma.**   37. _____

38. An overuse of **underlining** (italics) for emphasis should be avoided.   38. _____

39. The **contraction** of the words *have not* is written thus: *hav'ent.*   39. _____

40. Nonrestrictive clauses are always set off with **commas.**   40. _____

41. **Double quotation marks** are used around the name of a ship.   41. _____

42. A **comma** is used before the word *then* when it introduces a second clause.   42. _____

43. The prefix *semi-* always requires a **hyphen.**   43. _____

44. **No comma** is required in the following sentence: "Where do you wish to go?" he asked.   44. _____

45. A **dash** is a legitimate substitute for all other marks of punctuation.   45. _____

46. A **hyphen** is used between two parts of a written-out number from 21 to 99.   46. _____

47. Names of persons directly addressed are set off by a **comma** (or **commas**).   47. _____

48. Every introductory prepositional phrase is set off by a **comma.**   48. _____

49. An introductory adverbial clause is set off with a **comma.**   49. _____

50. A **colon** may be used instead of a **semicolon** between two independent clauses when the second
clause is an explanation of the first clause.   50. _____

62. PUNCTUATION: REVIEW

(Study P.)

Write **1** if the punctuation in brackets is **correct**.
Write **0** if it is **incorrect**.
(Use only one number in each blank.)

Example: The church bells[,] have been ringing all morning.   0

1. He found math difficult[;] but, because he worked so hard, he earned a *B*.   1. _____

2. The Messicks were late[,] their car battery having gone dead.   2. _____

3. I wondered what Shirley was doing[?]   3. _____

4. Dear Dr. Stanley[;] Thank you for your letter of May 10.   4. _____

5. Peter enjoyed inviting his friends[,] and preparing elaborate meals for them; however, most of his attempts were disasters.   5. _____

6. When the clerk brought out the red coat, Vera asked, "How much is it["?]   6. _____

7. I remembered Dad's remark: "I promised not to say, [']I told you so![']"   7. _____

8. "You may use my car," she said[,] "I won't be needing it today."   8. _____

9. A novella by Conrad, a short story by Lawrence, and some poems of Yeats[,] were all assigned for the last week of the semester.   9. _____

10. She arrived in Truro, Nova Scotia[,] last Saturday.   10. _____

11. The children's enthusiasm about going to the zoo was greater than our[']s.   11. _____

12. The relief workers specifically requested food, blankets, and childrens['] clothing.   12. _____

13. He opened his briefcase[,] he took out his notes and began to talk.   13. _____

14. Whenever he speaks, he uses too many *eh*[']s at the end of his sentences.   14. _____

15. Someone should tell his wife[;] the only person who can help him overcome this fault.   15. _____

16. The last employee to leave the office is responsible for the following[,] turning off all machines, extinguishing all lights, and locking all executives' office doors.   16. _____

17. Everywhere there were crowds shouting anti[-]American slogans.   17. _____

18. This is the game all Canada[']s been waiting for—the Vanier Cup.   18. _____

19. During the whole wretched ordeal of his trial[;] Charles Darnay remained outwardly calm.   19. _____

20. More than twenty minutes were cut from the original version of the film[,] the producers told neither the director nor the writer.   20. _____

21. December 3, 1966[,] is the date of my birth.   21. _____

22. The fugitive was located near Norwich, Ontario[,] in a deserted farmhouse.   22. _____

23. The temperature sinking fast as dusk approached[,] we decided to seek shelter for the night. 23. _____

24. MacArthur's forces landed at Inchon[;] thus cutting off the North Koreans.   24. _____

25. My only cousin[,] who is in the Canadian Armed Forces[,] is stationed in the Arctic.   25. _____

26. Any Canadian Armed Forces officer[,] who is stationed in the Arctic[,] receives extra pay.   26. _____

27. Good grief! Did she agree to that[?!]   27. _____

28. Heidi did not break the record in the marathon[,] she missed it by two-tenths of a second.   28. _____

29. Murphy's boss commended him on his frankness and spunk; then she fired Murphy.   29. _____

30. He wanted[,] to tell the truth[,] but lacked the courage.   30. _____

63. MECHANICS: CAPITALS

(Study M-2.)

Write **1** if the boldface words are **correct** in use or omission of capital letters.
Write **0** if they are **incorrect**.

Example: Cajuns speak a dialect of *french*.   0

1. They met at the **North Side Jewish Center.**   1. _____

2. My brother teaches **high school.**   2. _____

3. The *turkish* bath is closed.   3. _____

4. Mario's uncle is a Catholic **Priest.**   4. _____

5. When will **Parliament** convene?   5. _____

6. He is a **Graduate** of Trent.   6. _____

7. My daughter graduated from **McGill University.**   7. _____

8. He always disliked **Algebra.**   8. _____

9. Mars is the **god** of war.   9. _____

10. I greeted **Professor** Allen.   10. _____

11. She met three **Professors** today.   11. _____

12. "Do you live here?" **she** asked.   12. _____

13. I love the colors of **Fall.**   13. _____

14. The deaths were reported in **the Globe.**   14. _____

15. I was born in the **North.**   15. _____

16. Her **Aunt Miriam** has returned.   16. _____

17. He's late for his **economics** class.   17. _____

18. Jane was **President** of her club.   18. _____

19. Woods was promoted to **Major.**   19. _____

20. My **Grandfather** wrote to me.   20. _____

21. I enrolled in **english** and art.   21. _____

22. He began his letter with "My **Dear** Mrs. Johnson."   22. _____

23. He ended it with "Yours **Truly.**"   23. _____

24. We once lived in the American **South.**   24. _____

25. I passed German but failed **Calculus.**   25. _____

26. He entered **College** last fall.   26. _____

27. My **father** is an executive.   27. _____

28. I asked **Father** what he meant.   28. _____

29. He goes to **Pearson High School.**   29. _____

30. Has the **house** elected a speaker yet?   30. _____

31. The twins are now **Busines Majors.**   31. _____

32. The chess champion attends **Royal West Junior High School.**   32. _____

33. Emma is in *junior* high school.   33. _____

34. I spent the summer with my **Cousin.**   34. _____

35. Her favorite subject is *french*.   35. _____

36. The tourists visited the **Grand Canyon.**   36. _____

37. I drove *east* along Bloor.   37. _____

38. He enrolled in **Physics 2.**   38. _____

39. This is a **United Church.**   39. _____

40. I saw Sid (**What** is his last name?) downstairs.   40. _____

41. This is **NOT** my idea of fun.   41. _____

42. A box of *chinaware* was damaged.   42. _____

43. She earned a **Ph.D.** degree.   43. _____

44. The **World Series** had ended.   44. _____

45. She declared that charity is considered a **Christian** virtue.   45. _____

46. His father fought in the Korean *war*.   46. _____

47. The chairperson of the **Department of Computer Sciences** is Dr. MacIntosh.   47. _____

48. He said simply, "*my* name is Bond."   48. _____

49. "*I Meet Wayne*" is a chapter from a book by Scott Ellman.   49. _____

50. She spent her **Thanksgiving** vacation in Manitoba with her cousins.   50. _____

64. MECHANICS: CAPITALS

(Study M-2.)

In the first column, write the number of the **first correct** choice (**1** or **2**).
In the second column, write the number of the **second correct** choice (**3** or **4**).

Example: Wandering (1)*West* (2)*west,* Max met (3)*Milly* (4)*milly.*   _2_ _3_

1. Eaton's Department (1)*Store* (2)*store* is having a great sale on Italian (3)*Shoes.* (4)*shoes.*   1. ____ ____

2. Her (1)*Father* (2)*father* went (3)*North* (4)*north* on business.   2. ____ ____

3. The new (1)*College* (2)*college* is seeking a (3)*President* (4)*president.*   3. ____ ____

4. I was told to begin my letter with "My (1)*Dear* (2)*dear* (3)*Sir* (4)*sir.*"   4. ____ ____

5. I ended it with "Very (1)*Truly* (2)*truly* (3)*Yours* (4)*yours.*"   5. ____ ____

6. After (1)*Church* (2)*church* we walked across the Concordia (3)*Bridge* (4)*bridge.*   6. ____ ____

7. The (1)*Headwaiter* (2)*headwaiter* bowed deferentially to his (3)*Royal* (4)*royal* guests.   7. ____ ____

8. The young (1)*Lieutenant* (2)*lieutenant* prayed to the (3)*Lord* (4)*lord* for courage in the coming battle.   8. ____ ____

9. My (1)*Sister* (2)*sister* now lives in the (3)*East* (4)*east.*   9. ____ ____

10. The (1)*Prime Minister* (2)*prime minister* addresses the (3)*Commons* (4)*commons* to-morrow.   10. ____ ____

11. Edna Barney, (1)*M.D.* (2)*m.d.,* once taught (3)*Biology 4* (4)*biology 4.*   11. ____ ____

12. Dr. Galloway, (1)*Professor* (2)*professor* of (3)*English,* (4)*english,* is now on leave.   12. ____ ____

13. She always does well in (1)*French* (2)*french* and (3)*Math* (4)*math* courses.   13. ____ ____

14. "I'm also a graduate of Humber (1)*College,*" (2)*college,*" (3)*She* (4)*she* added.   14. ____ ____

15. The pastor of St. Paul's Anglican (1)*Church* (2)*church* is an (3)*Australian.* (4)*australian.*   15. ____ ____

16. Vera disagreed with the review of (1)*The* (2)*the* Wiz in (3)*The* (4)*the* Globe and Mail.   16. ____ ____

17. The club (1)*Secretary* (2)*secretary* said that the minutes of the meeting were "(3)*Almost* (4)*almost* complete."   17. ____ ____

18. The (1)*Girl Scout* (2)*girl scout* leader pointed out the (3)*Milky Way* (4)*milky way* to her troop.   18. ____ ____

19. She read *Language* (1)*In* (2)*in* Thought (3)*And* (4)*and* Action.   19. ____ ____

20. Her office is in (1)*Room* (2)*room* 218 of Hartley (3)*Hall.* (4)*hall.*   20. ____ ____

65. MECHANICS: NUMBERS AND ABBREVIATIONS

(Study M-4 and M-5.)

Write the number of the **correct** choice.

Example: That book is (1)*3* (2)*three* days overdue. _____2_____

1. (1)*1968* (2)*The year 1968* will be remembered as a turbulent time in North America. 1. _____

2. Several provinces have raised the drinking age to (1)*twenty-one.* (2)*21.* 2. _____

3. (1)*Prof.* (2)*Professor* Hilton teaches Oriental philosophy. 3. _____

4. Peterson was born in (1)*Ont.* (2)*Ontario.* 4. _____

5. Why is there no (1)*thirteenth* (2)*13th* floor in this building? 5. _____

6. The contest will be held at noon on (1)*Fri.* (2)*Friday.* 6. _____

7. When you are at the (1)*P.O.,* (2)*post office,* will you please buy some stamps for me? 7. _____

8. He worked for the T. Eaton (1)*Company* (2)*Co.* for ten years. 8. _____

9. She will tour Germany, (1)*Eng.,* (2)*England,* and France next summer. 9. _____

10. Robert Bailey, (1)*M.D.,* (2)*medical doctor,* is my physician. 10. _____

11. Frank jumped 7 meters, (1)*3* (2)*three* centimeters in last Saturday's meet. 11. _____

12. I had purchased coffee, flour, sugar, (1)*etc.* (2)*and other groceries.* 12. _____

13. He had made a dental appointment for (1)*3* (2)*three* o'clock. 13. _____

14. It was necessary for him to leave the campus by 2 (1)*P.M.* (2)*o'clock.* 14. _____

15. John's yearly income was (1)*$14,640* (2)*fourteen thousand six hundred forty dollars.* 15. _____

16. She graduated from high school on June (1)*6,* (2)*6th,* (3)*sixth,* 1984. 16. _____

17. He and his family moved to Nova Scotia last (1)*Feb.* (2)*February,* didn't they? 17. _____

18. Over (1)*900* (2)*nine hundred* students attend Cartier Junior High School. 18. _____

19. She was late in getting to her (1)*phys. ed.* (2)*physical education* class. 19. _____

20. Next year's convention will be held on April (1)*19,* (2)*19th,* (3)*nineteenth,* in Burlington. 20. _____

21. The petition contained (1)*2,983* (2)*two thousand nine hundred eighty-three* names. 21. _____

22. The lottery prize has reached an astonishing (1)*twenty-four million dollars.* (2)*$24 million.* 22. _____

23. Our neighbor had adopted a (1)*two-month-old* (2)*2-month-old* baby boy. 23. _____

24. (1)*The Reverend Harold Olson* (2)*Rev. Olson* was the speaker. 24. _____

25. The diagram was on (1)*pg.* (2)*page* 44. 25. _____

26. Mrs. Latimer will teach (1)*English* (2)*Eng.* next semester at Macdonald High School. 26. _____

27. Jody bought a puppy at the SPCA for (1)*Xmas.* (2)*Christmas.* 27. _____

28. I found the chart on page (1)*two hundred forty-one* (2)*241* very helpful. 28. _____

29. The plane expected from (1)*T.O. early this A.M.* (2)*Toronto early this morning* is late. 29. _____

30. The bus arrives at 10:55 A.M. and leaves at (1)*11:00* (2)*eleven* A.M. 30. _____

31. Ben earned (1)*three hundred dollars,* (2)*$300,* saved $80, and spent $40.   31. _____

32. Rachel's name was (1)*twenty-sixth* (2)*26th* on the list of high school graduates.   32. _____

33. The bad roads meant I had to use (1)*4-* (2)*four-*wheel drive.   33. _____

66. MECHANICS: CAPITALS, NUMBERS, AND ABBREVIATIONS

(Study M-2, M-4, and M-5.)

In the first column, write the number of the **first correct** choice (**1** or **2**).
In the second column, write the number of the **second correct** choice (**3** or **4**).

Example: There are only (1)*three* (2)*3* more days until (3)*Summer* (4)*summer* vacation.   <u> 1 </u>   <u> 4 </u>

1. Racial attitudes of many South African (1)*White* (2)*white* people must change if everyone there is to enjoy full (3)*Civil Rights.* (4)*civil rights.*   1. _____ _____

2. We have an (1)*Aborigine* (2)*aborigine* from Australia studying (3)*Engineering* (4)*engineering* here.   2. _____ _____

3. My (1)*Aunt* (2)*aunt* said her job was "(3)*Super* (4)*super* terrific."   3. _____ _____

4. "I expect," he said, "(1)*To* (2)*to* get an A in my (3)*Chem.* (4)*chemistry* class."   4. _____ _____

5. On June (1)*6* (2)*6th,* 1989, she spoke at D'Arcy McGee (3)*High School.* (4)*high school.*   5. _____ _____

6. The new college (1)*Rector* (2)*rector* greeted the (3)*Alumni.* (4)*alumni.*   6. _____ _____

7. A (1)*canadian* (2)*Canadian* flag flies from the top of the Bank of Commerce (3)*building* (4)*Building.*   7. _____ _____

8. The (1)*treasurer* (2)*Treasurer* of the (3)*Junior Accountants Club* (4)*junior accountants club* has absconded with our dues.   8. _____ _____

9. (1)*308* (2)*Three hundred eight* students passed the test, out of (3)*427* (4)*four hundred twenty-seven* who took it.   9. _____ _____

10. She likes her (1)*english* (2)*English* and (3)*science* (4)*Science* classes.   10. _____ _____

11. We knew that (1)*spring* (2)*Spring* in all her beauty would soon be smiling on the hills of eastern (3)*alberta.* (4)*Alberta.*   11. _____ _____

12. Industry in the (1)*West* (2)*west* is described in this month's (3)*Fortune* (4)*fortune* magazine.   12. _____ _____

13. Victor is going to take an (1)*english* (2)*English* course this semester instead of one in (3)*History.* (4)*history.*   13. _____ _____

14. She was happy; (1)*She* (2)*she* had reservations on the (3)*lurline.* (4)*Lurline.*   14. _____ _____

15. The new (1)*doctor* (2)*Doctor* has opened an office on Main (3)*Street.* (4)*street.*   15. _____ _____

16. The (1)*chinese* (2)*Chinese* student is (3)*18* (4)*eighteen* years old today.   16. _____ _____

17. I spent (1)*New Year's Day* (2)*new year's day* with (3)*mother.* (4)*Mother.*   17. _____ _____

18. Her (1)*French* (2)*french* teacher is going to the (3)*Orient.* (4)*orient.*   18. _____ _____

19. I need a (1)*Psychology* (2)*psychology* book from the (3)*Library.* (4)*library.*   19. _____ _____

20. The (1)*class* (2)*Class* of '75 honored the (3)*Dean of Men.* (4)*dean of men.*   20. _____ _____

21. Carla enrolled in (1)*Doctor* (2)*Dr.* Newell's history course; she is majoring in (3)*social science.* (4)*Social Science.*   21. _____ _____

22. Jim moved to eastern Saskatchewan; (1)*He* (2)*he* bought over (3)*400* (4)*four hundred* acres of land.   22. _____ _____

23. She knows (1)*four* (2)*4* students who are going to (3)*College* (4)*college* this fall.   23. _____ _____

24. The (1)*Conservative* (2)*conservative* government has decided that Canada will join the Organization of American (3)*States* (4)*states.*   24. _____ _____

25. After WW II, many (1)*inuit* (2)*Inuit* moved away from the remote parts of the (3)*North.* (4)*north.*   25. _____ _____

67. SPELLING: RECOGNIZING CORRECT FORMS

(Study S-1.)

Write the number of the **correctly spelled** word.

Example: A knowledge of (1)*grammer* (2)*grammar* is helpful.   <u>2</u>

1. (1)*Athletics* (2)*Atheletics* can be both healthful and enjoyable.   1. _____

2. I'm glad you didn't take it (1)*personaly.* (2)*personally.*   2. _____

3. No one thought that a romance would (1)*develope* (2)*develop* between those two.   3. _____

4. Your snapshot will never come out; the sun is (1)*shining* (2)*shinning* into your lens.   4. _____

5. Shakespeare's Iago is one of the classic (1)*villains* (2)*villians* of the stage.   5. _____

6. There are sins of commission and sins of (1)*ommission.* (2)*omission.*   6. _____

7. Her grandmother will be (1)*ninety* (2)*ninty* years old next week.   7. _____

8. The salary will depend on how (1)*competant* (2)*competent* the employee is.   8. _____

9. We (1)*persued* (2)*pursued* the pickpocket through the crowd.   9. _____

10. We canceled our plans because of the (1)*changeable* (2)*changable* summer weather.   10. _____

11. He offered several (1)*ridiculous* (2)*rediculous* excuses for his behavior.   11. _____

12. Her car will (1)*accomodate* (2)*accommodate* only five passengers.   12. _____

13. We Canadians can be proud of our (1)*achievements* (2)*achievmments* in peace-keeping.   13. _____

14. Do you (1)*beleive* (2)*believe* everything that you read in the newspaper?   14. _____

15. My husband and I are fortunate in having (1)*similar* (2)*similiar* tastes.   15. _____

16. She is an (1)*unusually* (2)*unusualy* gifted musician, isn't she?   16. _____

17. Carrying automobile insurance seems a (1)*necessary* (2)*neccessary* precaution.   17. _____

18. I find you strangely (1)*desirable.*(2)*desireable.*   18. _____

19. His (1)*couragous* (2)*courageous* act won for him much admiration from the associates.   19. _____

20. She is (1)*optomistic* (2)*optimistic* about her chances of passing the course.   20. _____

21. Despite Holmes's warning, Scotland Yard once more let Moriarty (1)*disappear* (2)*dissappear* from London.   21. _____

22. I had already (1)*payed* (2)*paid* my tuition for the fall semester.   22. _____

23. My adviser (1)*reccomended* (2)*recommended* my enrolling in an English course.   23. _____

24. Her future (1)*happiness* (2)*happyness* was very important to him.   24. _____

25. Two hunting (1)*knifes* (2)*knives* had been stolen from the trophy case.   25. _____

26. To be praised extravagantly always (1)*embarrasses* (2)*embarasses* him.   26. _____

27. (1)*Repitition* (2)*Repetition* can very easily become very, very monotonous.   27. _____

28. I had (1)*fulfilled* (2)*fullfilled* all the requirements for graduation.   28. _____

29. Because he was overly (1)*agressive* (2)*aggressive* he was not very popular.   29. _____

30. She was eager to (1)*receive* (2)*recieve* an A in the course.   30. _____

31. Vanessa was left to make the final (1)*arrangments* (2)*arrangements* for the funeral. 31. _____

32. I would have (1)*profited* (2)*profitted* greatly by taking his advice. 32. _____

33. He is (1)*occasionally* (2)*ocassionally* absent from class. 33. _____

34. I was sitting in my room when the incident (1)*occured* (2)*occurred* in the lobby. 34. _____

35. The work of Dian Fossey demonstrates that gorillas have more than just a (1)*primitive* (2)*primative* intelligence. 35. _____

36. The spelling errors in her paper were very (1)*noticable.* (2)*noticeable.* 36. _____

37. The school (1)*superintendent* (2)*superintendant* visited several classes. 37. _____

38. The (1)*principle* (2)*principal* introduced him to several of the teachers. 38. _____

39. The coach said, "Game conditions will (1)*seperate* (2)*separate* the men from the boys." 39. _____

40. What a great (1)*athlete* (2)*athelete* he is! 40. _____

41. She tried (1)*dying* (2)*dyeing* some of her sweaters another color. 41. _____

42. Little Jonathan is now going to (1)*kindegarten.* (2)*kindergarten.* 42. _____

43. Is it too late to save our (1)*enviroment?* (2)*environment?* 43. _____

44. She was (1)*disappointed* (2)*disapointed* about the outcome of the election. 44. _____

45. His (1)*sternness* (2)*sterness* seemed completely uncalled for. 45. _____

46. An (1)*undisceplined* (2)*undisciplined* childhood probably explained his wildness. 46. _____

47. Her lack of interest had become very (1)*apparent* (2)*apparant* to all of us. 47. _____

48. I suggest you find a good (1)*phychologist* (2)*psychologist* immediately. 48. _____

49. The arbitrator's solution seemed (1)*sensible.* (2)*sensable.* 49. _____

50. The (1)*sophomore* (2)*sophmore* class voted to sponsor a dance next month. 50. _____

51. The high school's star athlete was a very (1)*conscientous* (2)*conscientious* student. 51. _____

52. After school each day, he washed dishes in a downtown (1)*restaurant.* (2)*restuarant.* 52. _____

53. Thanks to my word processor, I never (1)*misspell* (2)*mispell* words. 53. _____

54. The (1)*occurrence* (2)*occurence* was reported in the student newspaper. 54. _____

55. He annoyed her by keeping time to the (1)*rythm* (2)*rhythm* of the music. 55. _____

56. I could only guess at the age and (1)*heigth* (2)*height* of the giant redwood tree. 56. _____

57. He earned extra money by repairing (1)*radios* (2)*radioes* during the summer. 57. _____

58. Filling out (1)*questionaires* (2)*questionnaires* proved to be very time-consuming. 58. _____

59. Robert's (1)*perseverance* (2)*perseverence* led to his ultimate success in the theater. 59. _____

60. She has a (1)*tendancy* (2)*tendency* to do her best work early in the day. 60. _____

61. Carla put the dress back, refusing to pay the (1)*outragious* (2)*outrageous* price. 61. _____

62. Her services had become (1)*indispensible* (2)*indispensable* to the firm. 62. _____

63. A reception was held for students having an (1)*excellent* (2)*excellant* scholastic record. 63. _____

64. Steven patiently explained the (1)*mathamatics* (2)*mathematics* of the experiment to me, but I was still lost. 64. _____

65. You will find no (1)*prejudice* (2)*predjudice* in our organization. 65. _____

66. The farmer was dependent on (1)*government* (2)*goverment* subsidy. 66. _____

67. (1)*Professor* (2)*Proffessor* Hacksaw won't accept late papers. 67. _____

68. We were told to (1)*proceed* (2)*procede* with our experiment. 68. _____

69. Nobody (1)*tries* (2)*trys* harder than Denis to be a good hockey player. 69. _____

70. Haven't you (1)*ommitted* (2)*omitted* the name of the club president? 70. _____

71. Too many (1)*unecessary* (2)*unnecessary* digressions spoiled the speech. 71. _____

72. Caldwell is (1)*suppose to* (2)*supposed to* deliver the lumber sometime today. 72. _____

73. You can say (1)*potatos* (2)*potatoes* two ways but spell it only one. 73. _____

74. The aging movie actress still imagined herself to be (1)*irresistible.* (2)*irresistable.* 74. _____

75. A minor accident occurred in the chemistry (1)*labratory.* (2)*laboratory.* 75. _____

76. It was always a (1)*priviledge* (2)*privilege* to listen to her talk. 76. _____

77. An (1)*erroneous* (2)*erronous* announcement appeared in the local newspaper. 77. _____

78. His (1)*curiosity* (2)*curiousity* led him into new areas of research. 78. _____

79. The king's son was completely bald; still, everyone said he was the heir (1)*aparent.* (2)*apparent.* 79. _____

80. Only (1)*amateur* (2)*amatuer* athletes may compete in this event. 80. _____

68. SPELLING: CORRECTING ERRORS

(Study S-1 and S-2.)

Twenty of the words below are misspelled (in addition to the sample).
After each **correct** word, write **1** in the narrow column and nothing in the wide column.
After each **misspelled** word, write **0** in the narrow column and the correct spelling in the wide column.

Example: hindrance	1		24. character		
Example: vacum	0	vacuum	25. adolescense		
1. tragedy			26. acquainted		
2. writing			27. nucleus		
3. anxious			28. pastime		
4. definite			29. catagory		
5. proceedure			30. fourty		
6. neice			31. amateur		
7. wierd			32. foreign		
8. familiar			33. business		
9. acknowlege			34. prejudice		
10. maneuver			35. nineth		
11. possession			36. entirely		
12. comparitive			37. finally		
13. truly			38. sergeant		
14. mischievious			39. persistant		
15. prevalent			40. parallel		
16. preceeding			41. acquire		
17. auxiliary			42. percieve		
18. conceivable			43. synonym		
19. irresistible			44. ectasy		
20. permissable			45. argument		
21. sacrilegious			46. exaggerate		
22. millionnaire			47. knowledge		
23. independent			48. exciteable		

49. exhilaration _____ _____

50. dissatisfied _____ _____

51. eighth _____ _____

52. maintenence _____ _____

53. existence _____ _____

54. playwright _____ _____

55. desperate _____ _____

56. schedule _____ _____

57. written _____ _____

58. management _____ _____

59. rhythm _____ _____

60. reminise _____ _____

69. SPELLING: CORRECTING ERRORS

(Study S-1 and S-2.)

On each line, **one** of the three words is misspelled.
In the first blank, write the column number of the **misspelled** word.
In the second blank, write the misspelled word **correctly.**

	Column 1	Column 2	Column 3	Number of Column Containing Misspelled Word	Misspelled Word Written Correctly
Example:	definate	opinion	ridiculous	1	definite
1.	surprise	guarantee	perserverence		
2.	forty	discription	condemn		
3.	criticism	comparitively	anxious		
4.	millionaire	indispensible	prevalent		
5.	acquired	pursue	auxillary		
6.	acknowledge	wierd	fictitious		
7.	apparant	maneuver	dropping		
8.	occurred	restaurant	changable		
9.	exaggerate	recieve	maintenance		
10.	ninty	ninth	foreign		
11.	argument	curiousity	separate		
12.	sensable	erroneous	shining		
13.	dilemma	tendency	questionaire		
14.	usually	sophmore	mischievous		
15.	priviledge	pastime	perform		
16.	forcibly	omission	exhileration		
17.	fasinating	government	reminisce		
18.	superintendent	intelligence	hypocricy		
19.	ecstasy	kindergarten	occurence		
20.	existance	perceive	omitted		

21.	synonym	sacrilegous	vengeance	_____	_____
22.	vacuum	noticable	amateur	_____	_____
23.	outrageous	unnecesary	repetition	_____	_____
24.	optimistic	dissatisfied	accomodate	_____	_____
25.	strength	tradgedy	sophomore	_____	_____
26.	misspelled	loveless	aquainted	_____	_____
27.	sieze	acquitted	adolescence	_____	_____
28.	irrelevant	primative	villain	_____	_____
29.	aggressive	knowlege	height	_____	_____
30.	writing	possession	competant	_____	_____

70. SPELLING: WORDS FREQUENTLY MISSPELLED

(Study S-2.)

In the numbered blank, write the number of the **letter missing** in the word: **1** for **a**, **2** for **e**, **3** for **i**, **4** for **o**. If **no letter is missing**, write **0**.

Example: gramm r	__1__	21. math matics	21. _____	
1. ben fited	1. _____	22. pre judice	22. _____	
2. tend ncy	2. _____	23. consist nt	23. _____	
3. occurr nce	3. _____	24. prim tive	24. _____	
4. pleas nt	4. _____	25. prev lent	25. _____	
5. defin te	5. _____	26. compar tive	26. _____	
6. permiss ble	6. _____	27. rep tition	27. _____	
7. opt mistic	7. _____	28. nec ssary	28. _____	
8. believ ble	8. _____	29. sacrileg ous	29. _____	
9. d scription	9. _____	30. compet nt	30. _____	
10. d vide	10. _____	31. desp rate	31. _____	
11. lov ble	11. _____	32. superintend nt	32. _____	
12. sim lar	12. _____	33. exist nce	33. _____	
13. appar nt	13. _____	34. excell nt	34. _____	
14. hindr nce	14. _____	35. sep rate	35. _____	
15. d spair	15. _____	36. independ nt	36. _____	
16. lab ratory	16. _____	37. irresist ble	37. _____	
17. indispens ble	17. _____	38. persever nce	38. _____	
18. famil ar	18. _____	39. opp rtunity	39. _____	
19. argu ment	19. _____	40. priv lege	40. _____	
20. forc bly	20. _____			

In the numbered blank,

write **1** if the missing letters are **ie;**
write **2** if the missing letters are **ei.**

Example: gr f	__1__	6. v n	6. _____	
1. h r	1. _____	7. ch f	7. _____	
2. ach ve	2. _____	8. l sure	8. _____	
3. dec ve	3. _____	9. th r	9. _____	
4. c ling	4. _____	10. w gh	10. _____	
5. w rd	5. _____	11. shr k	11. _____	

70.   SPELLING: WORDS FREQUENTLY MISSPELLED

12. r gn

13. bes ge

14. n ther

15. n ce

16. conc ve

12. _____

13. _____

14. _____

15. _____

16. _____

17. conc t

18. rec ve

19. bel ve

20. fr nd

17. _____

18. _____

19. _____

20. _____

71. USAGE: WORDS SIMILAR IN SOUND

(Study U.)

100%

Write the number of the **correct** choice.

Example: (1) *Your* (2) *You're* lovelier than ever. ___2___

1. Take my (1)*advice,* (2)*advise,* Julius; stay home today. 1. ___1___
2. I felt (1)*alright* (2)*all right* until I ate the soup. 2. ___2___
3. If you (1)*break* (2)*brake* the car gently, you won't feel a jolt. 3. ___2___
4. Camping trailers with (1)*canvas* (2)*canvass* tops are cooler than hardtop trailers. 4. ___1___
5. The diamond Richard bought for Elizabeth weighed more than three (1)*carets.* (2)*carats.* 5. ___2___
6. The cost of their (1)*cloths* (2)*clothes* would bankrupt a millionaire. 6. ___2___
7. The sandpaper was too (1)*course* (2)*coarse* for the job. 7. ___2___
8. Helping Allie with calculus was quite a (1)*decent* (2)*descent* gesture, don't you agree? 8. ___1___
9. This little (1)*device* (2)*devise* will revolutionize the computer industry. 9. ___1___
10. The new milk quotas angered the (1)*diary* (2)*dairy* industry. 10. ___2___
11. To (1)*elicit* (1)*illicit* student response, the teacher may ask affective as well as cognitive questions. 11. ___1___
12. She was one of the most (1)*imminent* (2)*eminent* educators of the decade. 12. ___2___
13. We knew that enemy troops would try to (1)*envelop* (2)*envelope* us. 13. ___1___
14. Kevin (1)*formerly* (2)*formally* had played for the Nordiques. 14. ___1___
15. Go (1)*fourth,* (2)*forth,* youngsters, and conquer the world. 15. ___2___
16. I hate to (1)*hear* (2)*here* what the dean is going to report. 16. ___1___
17. Sir, your notion is (1)*irrelevant* (2)*irreverent* to the issue. 17. ___1___
18. The ferry made the trip to the (1)*aisle* (2)*isle* in less than an hour. *WITHOUT RESPECT* 18. ___2___
19. She tried vainly to (1)*lessen* (2)*lesson* the tension in the house. 19. ___1___
20. The mourners wept as they filed (1)*passed* (2)*past* the bier. 20. ___2___
21. Morality is never simply a matter of (1)*personal* (2)*personnel* taste. 21. ___1___
22. The (1)*piece* (2)*peace* of the plane fell off in mid-flight. 22. ___1___
23. Her (1)*presents* (2)*presence* makes this a gala occasion. 23. ___2___
24. When the grand marshal gave the signal, the parade (1)*preceded.* (2)*proceeded.* 24. ___2___
25. Some people forsake the city to enjoy a (1)*quiet* (2)*quite* country life. 25. ___1___
26. Consider getting your degree as a (1)*rite* (2)*right* of passage. *ceremony* 26. ___1___
27. You can buy typing paper at any (1)*stationary* (2)*stationery* store. 27. ___2___
28. They knew better (1)*than* (2)*then* we did what the answer was. 28. ___1___
29. We caught a train that went (1)*thorough* (2)*through* to Sarnia. 29. ___2___
30. After weeks of miserable (1)*whether,* (2)*weather,* Scott gave up and went home. 30. ___2___

31. She is the first (1)**woman** (2)**women** to referee in this league.

31. ___1___

32. (1)**Your** (2)**You're** aware, aren't you, that the play is sold out?

32. ___2___

33. This dot-matrix printer will (1)**complement** (2)**compliment** your computer.

33. ___1___

72. USAGE: WORDS SIMILAR IN SOUND

(Study U.)

Write the number of the **correct** choice.

Example: William is (1)*to* (2)*too* (3)*two* clever for his own good.   ___2___

1. The rulers of the planet Zarkon will (1)*advice* (2)*advise* Earthlings not to land there.   1. _____

2. She signed the letter, "(1)*Respectively* (2)*Respectfully* yours."   2. _____

3. It is never (1)*all right* (2)*alright* for a driver to pass a stop sign.   3. _____

4. This handbag should (1)*complement* (2)*compliment* your new suit perfectly.   4. _____

5. Ned should be careful not to (1)*lose* (2)*loose* his temper so often.   5. _____

6. Go (1)*fourth* (2)*forth* and sin no more, the Bible says.   6. _____

7. I'd rather be rich (1)*then* (2)*than* poor.   7. _____

8. The (1)*course* (2)*coarse* for the marathon includes both flat and hilly terrain.   8. _____

9. Knowing that they have sufficient funds will (1)*lesson* (2)*lessen* their financial worries.   9. _____

10. The spectators fled when Marshall picked up the (1)*discuss.* (2)*discus.*   10. _____

11. Nobody (1)*accept* (2)*except* Gloria would stoop so low.   11. _____

12. If you write such things in your (1)*diary,* (2)*dairy,* keep it locked away.   12. _____

13. You will not find a better (1)*women* (2)*woman* on the entire staff.   13. _____

14. If you don't eat your spinach, Fiona, you won't get (1)*desert.* (2)*dessert.*   14. _____

15. She yearned for (1)*peace* (2)*piece* and tranquility in her daily life.   15. _____

16. If he (1)*past* (2)*passed* the physics test, it must have been easy.   16. _____

17. John Turner (1)*preceded* (2)*proceeded* Brian Mulroney as Prime Minister.   17. _____

18. The library copy of the magazine had lost (1)*it's* (2)*its* cover.   18. _____

19. He made his way (1)*thorough* (2)*through* the heavy underbrush.   19. _____

20. We had (1)*already* (2)*all ready* made arrangements to travel by bus.   20. _____

21. Can you name the (1)*capitols* (2)*capitals* of the ten provinces?   21. _____

22. I'm certain that (1)*your* (2)*you're* not intending to miss the concert tonight.   22. _____

23. His physical condition showed the (1)*effects* (2)*affects* of adequate rest and good food.   23. _____

24. I wouldn't walk (1)*further* (2)*farther* than necessary.   24. _____

25. We were (1)*quite* (2)*quiet* pleased with the results of our experiment.   25. _____

26. The steep (1)*descent* (2)*decent* down the mountain road was very hazardous.   26. _____

27. Shall we dress (1)*formally* (2)*formerly* for the Christmas Ball this year?   27. _____

28. To be a good teacher had become her (1)*principal* (2)*principle* concern.   28. _____

29. Are you certain that the bracelet is made of ten-(1)*carrot* (2)*caret* (3)*carat* gold?   29. _____

30. The Farkle family were (1)**altogether** (2)**all together** in the living room when their good friend and trusted neighbor made his surprise announcement.   30. _____

31. Shall I read the statement that (1)**precedes** (2)**proceeds** the examination questions?   31. _____

32. Would it not be better to make the dog's collar (1)**loser?** (2)**looser?**   32. _____

33. "I (1)**too** (2)**to** (3)**two** have a statement to make," she said.   33. _____

34. The bridge club stared in horror as the creature made (1)**its** (2)**it's** way toward them.   34. _____

35. The high-school (1)**principle** (2)**principal** spoke at the opening assembly.   35. _____

36. He said, "(1)**Their** (2)**There** (3)**They're** is no reason for you to wait."   36. _____

37. I could scarcely (1)**hear** (2)**here** what was being said because of the noise outside.   37. _____

38. "(1)**Whose** (2)**Who's** there?" she whispered hoarsely.   38. _____

39. "(1)**Accepting** (2)**Excepting** this award," she sobbed, "is an honor I deserve."   39. _____

40. They wanted a house with a separate (1)**dinning** (2)**dining** room.   40. _____

41. I decided to discuss my problem with the (1)**personnel** (2)**personal** manager.   41. _____

42. She had made up her mind to buy a new suit of (1)**cloths.** (2)**clothes.**   42. _____

43. The mere (1)**cite** (2)**sight** (3)**site** of Juliet made his heart soar.   43. _____

44. I hope to install a (1)**device** (2)**devise** that will serve as a burglar alarm.   44. _____

45. The new teacher was asked to (1)**consul** (2)**counsel** (3)**council** thirty-five students.   45. _____

46. I was willing to pay 6 percent interest on the unpaid (1)**principle.** (2)**principal.**   46. _____

47. His words were vulgar and his manners (1)**course.** (2)**coarse.**   47. _____

48. Lay your books on the table; (1)**then** (2)**than** we'll make plans for the evening.   48. _____

49. Will people be standing in the (1)**isles** (2)**aisles** at the dedication ceremony?   49. _____

50. Parts of the document were immaterial and (1)**irrelevant.** (2)**irreverent.**   50. _____

51. "Sad movies always (1)**effect** (2)**affect** me this way," he said, laughing.   51. _____

52. She could not decide (1)**whether** (2)**weather** or not to go back to work.   52. _____

53. The president suggested a (1)**canvas** (2)**canvass** of the members of the organization.   53. _____

54. He was obviously (1)**effected** (2)**affected** by the beauty of his surroundings.   54. _____

55. As children, we played a game to see who could stand (1)**stationary** (2)**stationery** for the longest time.   55. _____

56. I (1)**complimented** (2)**complemented** him on his extraordinary presence of mind.   56. _____

57. He is very (1)**through** (2)**thorough** and painstaking in all that he does.   57. _____

58. Jonathan had the (1)**presence** (2)**presents** of mind to make a sharp right turn and step on the accelerator.   58. _____

59. They started out alone on a dreary trip across the (1)**dessert.** (2)**desert.**   59. _____

60. This was another (1)**instance** (2)**instants** of his kindness and generosity.   60. _____

61. Two (1)**woman** (2)**women** and two men were on the committee.   61. _____

62. Dr. McBride is a distinguished and (1)**eminent** (2)**imminent** member of the faculty.   62. _____

63. We were (1)**already** (2)**all ready** to go on the pony ride when the rains came.   63. _____

64. The teacher had reported the matter to the (1)**principal.** (2)**principle.**   64. _____

65. It's obvious that (1)**there** (2)**they're** (3)**their** unwilling to listen to reason.   65. _____

66. The measure passed without a (1)*fourth* (2)*forth* of the arguments being presented.   66. _____

67. I was certain that he would not (1)*desert* (2)*dessert* the ship.   67. _____

68. The track coach told me that he wanted to (1)*discus* (2)*discuss* my performance at the last meet.   68. _____

69. The moving object had now become (1)*stationary.* (2)*stationery.*   69. _____

70. "What is (1)*you're* (2)*your* candid opinion?" she asked.   70. _____

71. "(1)*Who's* (2)*Whose* your friend in the yellow car?" he asked.   71. _____

72. In the mountains we quickly felt the (1)*affects* (2)*effects* of a change in elevation.   72. _____

73. She was very (1)*clothes* (2)*close* to winning when she withdrew from competition.   73. _____

74. Her attitude was impertinent and (1)*irreverent.* (2)*irrelevant.*   74. _____

75. We suspected that an upset in our plans was (1)*eminent.* (2)*imminent.*   75. _____

76. She is a (1)*notable* (2)*notorious* liar.   76. _____

77. Come (1)*forth* (2)*fourth* and you won't win any medals.   77. _____

78. I could never (1)*quite* (2)*quiet* understand her motives.   78. _____

79. In later life, Toto was appointed honorary (1)*council* (2)*consul* (3)*counsel* for the Land of Oz.   79. _____

80. "(1)*You're* (2)*Your* most certainly wrong!" he exclaimed.   80. _____

73. USAGE: WORD CHOICE

(Study U.)

Write the number of the **correct** choice. (Formal standard English is intended.)

Example: Willa wanted the doll very (1)*much.* (2)*badly.*   __1__

1. He keeps trying to (1)*discover* (2)*invent* a better mousetrap.   1. _____

2. Your essay has (1)*its* (2)*it's* faults, but it makes some excellent points too.   2. _____

3. A tall tree has fallen and is (1)*laying* (2)*lying* across the highway.   3. _____

4. The exhaust fumes made him feel (1)*nauseated* (2)*nauseous.*   4. _____

5. With capital punishment, the wrong person might be (1)*hung.* (2)*hanged.*   5. _____

6. I could not help (1)*but feel* (2)*feeling* sad when I read the book about the whales.   6. _____

7. Did you ask if he will (1)*let* (2)*leave* you open a charge account?   7. _____

8. She thought that she had paid (1)*to* (2)*too* (3)*two* much for her television set.   8. _____

9. I found that the bag of potatoes had (1)*busted* (2)*burst* (3)*bursted* open.   9. _____

10. We were surprised (1)*somewhat* (2)*some* at his sudden outburst.   10. _____

11. The old inn is only a short (1)*ways* (2)*way* down the road.   11. _____

12. Will the new legislation (1)*affect* (2)*effect* your business?   12. _____

13. I really shouldn't have (1)*excepted* (2)*accepted* his generous offer of help.   13. _____

14. We were (1)*real* (2)*very* pleased they came to the rodeo.   14. _____

15. You and Michael will have to share the book (1)*between* (2)*among* you.   15. _____

16. We heard the same report (1)*everywhere* (2)*everyplace* we went.   16. _____

17. I knew that it would be (1)*alright* (2)*all right* for us to go the matinee.   17. _____

18. That the people are sovereign is the first (1)*principle* (2)*principal* of a democratic society.   18. _____

19. As soon as he had (1)*affected* (2)*effected* his release, he telephoned her.   19. _____

20. Do (1)*try to* (2)*try and* spend the night with us when you are in town.   20. _____

21. I suspected that Sue's mother was (1)*most* (2)*almost* at the end of her patience.   21. _____

22. "Shooting innocent civilians is one of war's most (1)*amoral* (2)*immoral* acts," the minister said.   22. _____

23. The alfalfa milkshake may taste awful, but it is (1)*healthy.* (2)*healthful.*   23. _____

24. Sarah always (1)*lies* (2)*lays* down to rest after an unusual exertion.   24. _____

25. Timothy (1)*lay* (2)*laid* new linoleum on the floor of the recreation room last week.   25. _____

26. (1)*As for me,* (2)*As for my part,* I particularly dislike television commercials.   26. _____

27. My reading stories (1)*aloud* (2)*out loud* delighted the children.   27. _____

28. When my dog wants (1)*in,* (2)*to come in,* she barks and whines.   28. _____

29. I went (1)*right* (2)*directly* to the cafeteria after my last class.   29. _____

30. The (1)*amount* (2)*number* of trees needed to produce a single book should humble any author.   30. _____

31. We were (1)**altogether** (2)**all together** satisfied with the arrangements.   31. _____

32. I remain (1)**respectively** (2)**respectfully** yours, Clyde Barrow.   32. _____

33. The Allies' scheme was (1)**practicable** (2)**practical** but dangerous.   33. _____

34. I (1)**had ought** (2)**ought** to have let her know the time of my arrival.   34. _____

35. They had (1)**already** (2)**all ready** canceled their reservations.   35. _____

36. The dog has (1)**laid** (2)**lain** on the front steps all morning.   36. _____

37. Caroline is an (1)**alumnus** (2)**alumna** of Concordia.   37. _____

38. Chokies taste good (1)**like** (2)**as** a carcinogen should.   38. _____

39. She (1)**suspected** (2)**suspicioned** her dog of having stolen the package of meat.   39. _____

40. He (1)**adopted** (2)**adapted** readily to a change in his environment.   40. _____

41. She was not (1)**enthused** (2)**enthusiastic** about his plan to buy a ranch.   41. _____

42. Will you be sure to (1)**contact** (2)**get in touch with** me tomorrow?   42. _____

43. He (1)**seldom ever** (2)**hardly ever** writes to his sister.   43. _____

44. Anna was (1)**besides** (2)**beside** herself with anger.   44. _____

45. (1)**Hadn't I ought** (2)**Ought I not** to report the incident at once?   45. _____

46. Buck is throwing the ball (1)**good** (2)**well** this spring.   46. _____

47. Do (1)**set** (2)**sit** down and tell me all about your summer vacation.   47. _____

48. The man was (1)**annoyed** (2)**aggravated** by the noise made by his neighbor's children.   48. _____

49. I believe that she is living (1)**someplace** (2)**somewhere** in South America.   49. _____

50. One reason for his poor health is (1)**because** (2)**that** he doesn't get enough sleep.   50. _____

51. The curtain was about to (1)**raise** (2)**rise** on the last act of the senior play.   51. _____

52. He exclaimed, "I (1)**couldn't hardly** (2)**could hardly** believe my ears!"   52. _____

53. She lived in constant fear of (1)**losing** (2)**loosing** her passport.   53. _____

54. Mother was (1)**sure** (2)**surely** happy when I told her that I would be home for Christmas.   54. _____

55. Exhausted from their cold plunge into the ocean, the swimmers were (1)**laying** (2)**lying** on the beach.   55. _____

56. The camp is just a few miles (1)**further** (2)**farther** along this trail.   56. _____

57. I wrote to the registrar (1)**in regard to** (2)**in regards to** my missing transcript.   57. _____

58. The passengers were instructed to fasten (1)**they're** (2)**their** (3)**there** seat belts.   58. _____

59. Judge Bean sentenced Black Bart to be (1)**hanged** (2)**hung** immediately after the trial.   59. _____

60. She wanted (1)**badly** (2)**very much** to stay in Japan for a month of sightseeing.   60. _____

74. USAGE: WORD CHOICE

(Study U.)

Write **1** if the boldface expression is **correct**.
Write **0** if it is **incorrect**.
(Formal standard English is intended.)

Example: The car's fender was dented and **it's** windshield was cracked.   **0**

1. **Those sort** of books are expensive.   1. _____
2. He played **like** he was inspired.   2. _____
3. Standards of living have **raised.**   3. _____
4. Some dogs look **like** their masters.   4. _____
5. You **hadn't ought** to sneak into the show.   5. _____
6. **It's** time for us to go.   6. _____
7. You **too** can afford such a car.   7. _____
8. We were **plenty** disappointed with the Meech Lake Accord.   8. _____
9. I couldn't find John **anyplace.**   9. _____
10. He parked his car **in back of** Deborah's house.   10. _____
11. The cornerstone was being **laid.**   11. _____
12. **Irregardless** of the result, you did your best.   12. _____
13. Will he **raise** the sales tax?   13. _____
14. Try to keep him **off of** the pier.   14. _____
15. I **suspicioned** him of dishonesty.   15. _____
16. He **rarely ever** arrives late.   16. _____
17. Just try **and** stop me!   17. _____
18. Her success was **due to** hard work and persistence.   18. _____
19. I'm to go too, **aren't I?**   19. _____
20. **They're** house is now for sale.   20. _____
21. Julia and **myself** decided to open a dress shop.   21. _____
22. The club has lost **its** president.   22. _____
23. Susan is **awfully** happy.   23. _____
24. Did he **lay** awake last night?   24. _____
25. She is not **enthused** about tennis.   25. _____
26. Bob **laid** the carpet in the hallway.   26. _____
27. We **sure** hope you are able to go.   27. _____
28. He **better** get here before noon.   28. _____
29. She is a **real** reliable person.   29. _____
30. He **has been laying** in the hammock all morning.   30. _____
31. I admire **that kind** of initiative.   31. _____
32. He has **plenty** of opportunities for earning money.   32. _____
33. He was **plenty** worried at not hearing from her.   33. _____
34. David looked **like** he wanted to avoid her.   34. _____
35. **Most** all her friends sent cards.   35. _____
36. The damage was **nowhere near** as great as I thought it might be.   36. _____
37. He always did **good** in English.   37. _____
38. She resigned **because of** illness.   38. _____
39. He **lay** in bed until noon.   39. _____
40. Max has **less** enemies than Sam.   40. _____
41. He **laid** his hammer on the porch.   41. _____
42. He has a long **way** to go tonight.   42. _____
43. Did he **loose** his wallet?   43. _____
44. She walked **like** she was in pain.   44. _____
45. He told the dog to **lay** down.   45. _____
46. Who were the **principals** in the company?   46. _____
47. His finances are in bad **shape.**   47. _____
48. Have you written **in regards to** an appointment?   48. _____
49. Elaine **adopted** her novel for television.   49. _____
50. Damp weather **affects** her sinuses.   50. _____

75. USAGE: WORD CHOICE

(Study U.)

Write the number of the **correct** choice. (Formal standard English is intended.)

Example: Fix it (1)**anyways** (2)**any way** you can.   <u>2</u>

1. The book's author was (1)**censored** (2)**censured** for his views.   1. _____

2. You may borrow (1)**any one** (2)**anyone** of my books if you promise to return it.   2. _____

3. Compared (1)**to** (2)**with** the Argos, the Lions have a weaker defense but a stronger offense.   3. _____

4. The figure of Venus de Milo is an excellent example of (1)**classic** (2)**classical** sculpture.   4. _____

5. He should (1)**of** (2)**have** notified his hostess of his change in plans.   5. _____

6. The linebacking unit was (1)**composed** (2)**comprised** of Taylor, Marshall, and Burt.   6. _____

7. Be (1)**sure to** (2)**sure and** write to us when you arrive in New Brunswick.   7. _____

8. They invited no one to their wedding (1)**except** (2)**accept** their parents.   8. _____

9. (1)**Regardless** (2)**Irregardless** of difficulties, he will complete the project.   9. _____

10. The reason I changed my mind was (1)**because** (2)**that** she was persistent.   10. _____

11. The referee was completely (1)**uninterested** (2)**disinterested** and completely dedicated.   11. _____

12. The three children tried to outrun (1)**each other.** (2)**one another.**   12. _____

13. Early rainstorms had (1)**raised** (2)**risen** the level of the lake.   13. _____

14. (1)**Everyplace** (2)**Everywhere** we went, we encountered hospitable people.   14. _____

15. He is very (1)**enthusiastic** (2)**enthused** about playing the part of the villain.   15. _____

16. I spoke to the agent about (1)**ensuring** (2)**insuring** the cottage.   16. _____

17. I'm a very stupid person, (1)**aren't I?** (2)**am I not?** (3)**ain't I?**   17. _____

18. We could not ship by air the (1)**number** (2)**amount** of cartons that the company ordered.   18. _____

19. The vase was (1)**setting** (2)**sitting** on the table where I had left it.   19. _____

20. Her brilliant performance was (1)**due to** (2)**because of** talent and ability.   20. _____

21. Bob and (1)**myself** (2)**I** will spend the summer on the Prairies.   21. _____

22. Man's first step on the moon was a (1)**historic** (2)**historical** moment in the exploration of space.   22. _____

23. We had (1)**less** (2)**fewer** problems than we had anticipated.   23. _____

24. When the playground director arrived, Tom was (1)**nowheres** (2)**nowhere** to be found.   24. _____

25. The teenagers spent the day (1)**laying** (2)**lying** on the beach in the sun.   25. _____

26. If you (1)**lose** (2)**loose** your driver's license, report the loss at once.   26. _____

27. He followed directions just (1)**like** (2)**as** he had been instructed.   27. _____

28. (1)**Due to** (2)**Because of** uncertain weather, our flight had been canceled.   28. _____

29. He was put on probation (1)**due to** (2)**because of** habitual truancy.   29. _____

30. A (1)**rising** (2)**raising** barometer indicated a marked change in the weather.   30. _____

31. The child's body showed obvious (1)*effects* (2)*affects* of malnutrition.   31. _____

32. The quick snack he had before dinner (1)*lessoned* (2)*lessened* his hunger.   32. _____

33. The new ruling will (1)*affect* (2)*effect* all entering students this fall.   33. _____

34. The statue (1)*sits* (2)*sets* on a high pedestal opposite the entrance to the park.   34. _____

35. I walked (1)*past* (2)*passed* her without speaking.   35. _____

36. The loud ticking of the clock proved to be very (1)*aggravating* (2)*annoying* to her.   36. _____

37. A cloud of smoke was (1)*rising* (2)*raising* from the distant hillside.   37. _____

38. Detective Chandler gave the apartment a (1)*through* (2)*thorough* inspection.   38. _____

39. The leader's efforts to find them had been (1)*altogether* (2)*all together* praiseworthy.   39. _____

40. People considered him a man of high (1)*principles.* (2)*principals.*   40. _____

41. Excuse me, Your Honor, but I have to (1)*utilize* (2)*use* the bathroom.   41. _____

42. Her attitude toward the problem was quite different (1)*from* (2)*than* his.   42. _____

43. He (1)*could hardly* (2)*couldn't hardly* make his way up the steep incline.   43. _____

44. The test was (1)*not nearly* (2)*nowhere near* as difficult as she expected it to be.   44. _____

45. He receives (1)*less* (2)*fewer* telephone calls than I do.   45. _____

46. She wanted to believe that there was (1)*no such a* (2)*no such* word as *can't.*   46. _____

47. We had no doubt (1)*but what* (2)*that* he would one day become a college principal.   47. _____

48. I shall let you know our decision (1)*within* (2)*inside of* an hour.   48. _____

49. The doctors worked feverishly to remove the (1)*piece* (2)*peace* of shrapnel from the infantryman's leg.   49. _____

50. The rank of captain in the navy corresponds (1)*to* (2)*with* that of colonel in the army.   50. _____

51. Let the documents (1)*lie* (2)*lay* on the table where he left them.   51. _____

52. We invited (1)*the Reverend Mr. Englund* (2)*Reverend Englund* to come as our guest.   52. _____

53. The speakers were much better informed about the subject (1)*then* (2)*than* I was.   53. _____

54. I am very late in handling in this paper, (1)*aren't I?* (2)*am I not?*   54. _____

55. My inability to pay was (1)*due to* (2)*because of* a shortage of funds.   55. _____

56. I, (1)*to,* (2)*too,* was in agreement with the speaker's remarks about the controversy.   56. _____

57. She was (1)*very much* (2)*plenty* upset about her low scholastic average.   57. _____

58. He was obviously (1)*two* (2)*to* (3)*too* stunned to speak.   58. _____

59. (1)*Any more* (2)*Anymore* behavior like that, young man, and you'll go straight to bed.   59. _____

60. Shouldn't you (1)*lay* (2)*lie* down after your long walk?   60. _____

76. USAGE: WORD CHOICE

(Study U.)

Write **1** if the boldface expression is **correct.**
Write **0** if it is **incorrect.**
(Formal standard English is intended.)

Example: The day was *like* a bad dream.   __1__

1. A lion hunting its prey is *immoral.*   1. _____
2. The bus was *already* to leave.   2. _____
3. They *normally always* win.   3. _____
4. Has *any one* here seen Betty?   4. _____
5. *Almost* all my friends came.   5. _____
6. The hum of the air conditioner was *continual.*   6. _____
7. The villain is usually *hanged.*   7. _____
8. The car runs *good* now.   8. _____
9. She is *too* young to understand.   9. _____
10. *Irregardless* of his shortcomings, she loves him.   10. _____
11. Where is my bankbook *at*?   11. _____
12. He had no intention of jumping *off of* the bridge.   12. _____
13. The salesperson *contacted* him.   13. _____
14. The sun will *hopefully* shine tomorrow.   14. _____
15. *They're* financial obligations had become too heavy for them.   15. _____
16. The harshness of his voice proved *irritating* to me.   16. _____
17. His chances looked *good.*   17. _____
18. The twins frequently wear *one another's* clothes.   18. _____
19. A twisted branch was *laying* across our path.   19. _____
20. She was *disinterested* in the boring play.   20. _____
21. Cheryl was *enthused* about being on the basketball team.   21. _____
22. The rink holds *less* then six hundred people.   22. _____

23. The conflicting groups finally *effected* a compromise.   23. _____
24. Kate was *somewhat* annoyed.   24. _____
25. Sam *differs from* Gina about the need for more taxes.   25. _____
26. I meant to *lay* down for an hour.   26. _____
27. Let's think *further* about it.   27. _____
28. What are you looking *at*?   28. _____
29. He enjoys the *healthy* food we serve.   29. _____
30. The children had walked to school by *theirselves.*   30. _____
31. I could not help *but feel* sorry for the two culprits.   31. _____
32. Her story was *incredulous.*   32. _____
33. It is a *most unique* situation.   33. _____
34. He had *already* departed.   34. _____
35. Theirs was a *lose* arrangement.   35. _____
36. *Due to* the pollution levels, the city banned incinerators.   36. _____
37. The three girls chatted with *each other* about the party.   37. _____
38. First and second honors were given to John and Harold, *respectively.*   38. _____
39. I was *mad* with love for her.   39. _____
40. Only Alex and *myself* attended the meeting.   40. _____
41. She was *terribly* pleased at winning the contest.   41. _____
42. *Their* is always another game.   42. _____
43. The red rug had *lain* on the floor for ten years.   43. _____
44. Let's hope the vote will be sooner *then* later.   44. _____
45. Fillion *lead* the race from start to finish.   45. _____

46. He *implied* that I was at fault.   46. _____   49. *They're* not at home today.   49. _____

47. *Lie* down your heavy load.   47. _____   50. We ventured *further* into the woods.   50. _____

48. The cost of living keeps *rising.*   48. _____

77. USAGE: WORD CHOICE

(Study U.)

Write **1** if the boldface expression is **correct.**
Write **0** if it is **incorrect.**
(Formal standard English is intended.)

Example: Malina **sure** could sew. ___0___

1. No one in Canada has been **hanged** for many years. 1. _____

2. The child seemed to be **healthy.** 2. _____

3. She died **due to** pneumonia. 3. _____

4. Jaime **emigrated** from Mexico in 1988. 4. _____

5. The phone rang **continually.** 5. _____

6. We leave **inside** of five minutes. 6. _____

7. The dig reached the bottom **strata.** 7. _____

8. His reasons are different **than** mine. 8. _____

9. I was **continually** interrupted. 9. _____

10. **Being as** I was early, I waited. 10. _____

11. He bought cake, soda, **and etc.** 11. _____

12. June has **less** days than July. 12. _____

13. Be **sure and** write if you get work. 13. _____

14. He hiked **farther** than I. 14. _____

15. Swimming is **healthful** exercise. 15. _____

16. They **seldom ever** meet. 16. _____

17. He lost **due to** inexperience. 17. _____

18. It took more than an hour to **climb up** Mount Abraham. 18. _____

19. I **set** my packages on the table. 19. _____

20. Bell **discovered** the telephone. 20. _____

21. Her **folks** will be here tomorrow. 21. _____

22. I shall **contact** my attorney. 22. _____

23. He faltered **because of** fatigue. 23. _____

24. He fell **off** the ladder. 24. _____

25. I am **nowhere near** ready to go. 25. _____

26. Sue's balloon had **bursted.** 26. _____

27. The temple **sits** on a high hill. 27. _____

28. I **can but** sympathize with him. 28. _____

29. I asked **in regards to** my check. 29. _____

30. I am **enthused** about this job. 30. _____

31. Biff is a **hardy-type** fellow. 31. _____

32. I **see where** the school bonds failed to pass. 32. _____

33. The reason she stutters is **because** she's nervous. 33. _____

34. He **cannot help but** be grateful for the help he has received. 34. _____

35. The cat has been **lying** on the hearth all afternoon. 35. _____

36. I'm sure that he will be **O.K.** 36. _____

37. The instructor's lack of comments **aggravated** her. 37. _____

38. He **rose** petunias as a hobby. 38. _____

39. She does **well** in examinations. 39. _____

40. The red dress looks **good** on her. 40. _____

41. Dr. Freud remained **mad** for years. 41. _____

42. I looked **everyplace** for my pen. 42. _____

43. Rivard was a **notable** public enemy. 43. _____

44. I **laid** my purse on the counter. 44. _____

45. The class was **all together** bored by the film. 45. _____

46. No modern playwright can be **compared to** Shakespeare. 46. _____

47. All roads lead there. Take **anyone.** 47. _____

48. When offered beer and wine, I choose the **latter.** 48. _____

49. We will **except** you from the rule. 49. _____

50. Is this test **verbal** or written? 50. _____

78. USAGE: WORD CHOICE

(Study U.)

Write **1** if the sentence is **correct**.
Write **0** if the sentence is **incorrect;** then write the correct version of the misused word in the second column.

Example: Its been a unique experience.   <u> 0 </u>   <u> It's </u>

1. Some people drive their cars like everyone else on the road were a sworn enemy.   1. ___ _____

2. We were altogether surprised when little Brian decided to take a nap.   2. ___ _____

3. There were far less campers at Camp Walletmaker that summer than its bunkhouses could hold.   3. ___ _____

4. We wanted to lay in the sun for a week and work on our tans.   4. ___ _____

5. Being jolted by 50 volts had little apparent affect on Harold, who insisted it had brightened up his day.   5. ___ _____

6. They laid the new floor in the kitchen in less than a day.   6. ___ _____

7. Parker said it was alright with him to put anchovies on the pizza but implied that he was just being polite.   7. ___ _____

8. Irregardless of my grades, I'm an excellent writer, except for word usage.   8. ___ _____

9. Keep your principles and you'll seldom ever regret it.   9. ___ _____

10. Making usage errors is truly aggravating, especially when someone cites an authority to prove you are wrong.   10. ___ _____

11. I sometimes lose track of the time when I am besides a beautiful thing.   11. ___ _____

12. We were far too credible about the investment, and that's how we lost our capital.   12. ___ _____

13. He better get to class on time; Professor Morrison is apt to complain if he's late again.   13. ___ _____

14. The judge was uninterested; she wished to determine only if the complaint were a genuine instance of discrimination.   14. ___ _____

15. Your absolutely right to go to traffic court and dispute the ticket.   15. ___ _____

16. Providing that she doesn't lose sight of her objective, she's a good bet to make the team.   16. ___ _____

17. When we saw that the restaurant was a little further down the road, our morale greatly improved.   17. ___ _____

18. Lie your head on my shoulder so that you can rest.   18. ___ _____

19. This sort of fish is far more tastier than any other.   19. ___ _____

20. We were far too close to the refineries; I began to feel nauseous.   20. ___ _____

79. BEYOND THE SENTENCE: PARAGRAPH DEVELOPMENT

(Study B-1.)

Underline the **topic sentence** of each paragraph. Then, in the blank at the end of the paragraph, write the number of the **method** used to develop the topic sentence:

1. facts or examples   3. definition
2. reasons   4. comparison or contrast

1. Every society tries to produce a prevalent psychological type that will best serve its ends, and that type is always prone to certain emotional malfunctions. In early capitalism, which was a producing society, the ideal type was acquisitive, fanatically devoted to hard work and fiercely repressive of sex. The emotional malfunctions to which this type was liable were hysteria and obsession. Later capitalism, today's capitalism, is a consuming society, and the psychological type it strives to create, in order to build up the largest possible markets, is shallow, easily swayed and characterized much more by self-infatuation than self-respect. The emotional malfunction of this type is narcissism.

—Margaret Halsey   1. _____

2. Now, to be properly enjoyed, a walking tour should be gone upon alone. If you go in a company, or even in pairs, it is no longer a walking tour in anything but name; it is something else and more in the nature of a picnic. A walking tour should be gone upon alone, because freedom is of the essence; because you should be able to stop and go on, and follow this way and that, as the freak takes you; and because you must have your own pace, and neither trot alongside a champion walker, nor mince in time with a girl. And then you must be open to all impressions and let your thoughts take color from what you see. You should be as a pipe for any wind to play upon. "I cannot see the wit," says Hazlitt, "of walking and talking at the same time. When I am in the country, I wish to vegetate like the country"—which is the gist of all that can be said upon the matter. There should be no cackle of voices at your elbow to jar on the meditative silence of the morning. And so long as a man is reasoning he cannot surrender himself to that fine intoxication that comes of much motion in the open air, that begins in a sort of dazzle and sluggishness of the brain, and ends in a peace that passes comprehension.

—Robert Louis Stevenson   2. _____

3. If you have any doubt of what a word means, look it up. Learn its etymology and notice what curious branches its original root has put forth. See if it has any other meanings that you didn't know it had. Master the small gradations between words which seem to be synonyms. What is the difference between "cajole," "wheedle," "blandish," and "coax"? An excellent guide to these nuances is *Webster's Dictionary of Synonyms.*

—William Zinsser   3. _____

4. The most essential distinction between athletics and education lies in the institution's own interest in the athlete as distinguished from its interest in its other students. Universities attract students in order to teach them what they do not already know; they recruit athletes only when they are already proficient. Students are educated for something which will be useful to them and to society after graduation; athletes are required to spend their time on activities the usefulness of which disappears upon graduation or soon thereafter. Universities exist to do what they can for students; athletes are recruited for what they can do for the universities. This makes the operation of the athletic program in which recruited players are used basically different from an educational interest of colleges and universities.

—Harold W. Stoke   4. _____

5.   Any education that matters is *liberal.* All the saving truths and healing graces that distinguish a good education from a bad one or a full education from a half-empty one are contained in that word. Whatever ups and down the term *"liberal"* suffers in the political vocabulary, it soars above all controversy in the educational world. In the blackest pits of pedagogy the squirming victim has only to ask, "What's liberal about this?" to shame his persecutors. In times past a liberal education set off a free man from a slave or a gentleman from laborers and artisans. It now distinguishes whatever nourishes the mind and spirit from the training which is merely practical or professional or from trivialities which are not training at all. Such an education involves a combination of knowledge, skills, and standards.

—Alan Simpson   5.   _____

6.   The fictional urge is basic. Humans dream in stories, daydream in stories; express hope for the future, account for the present, and recapture the past in stories. Fictional literature is an extension of life. It begins in tale telling, assumes widely divergent forms in different times and cultures, feeds upon itself in imitation or rejections of its constantly changing past, and takes specific shape in the print of an individual work.

—Northrop Frye   6.   _____

7.   What, then, is thinking? To begin with, it is a purposeful mental activity over which we exercise some control. *Control* is the key word. Just as sitting in the driver's seat of a car becomes driving only when we take the steering wheel in hand and control the car's movement, so our mind's movements become thinking only when we direct them.

—Vincent Ryan Ruggiero   7.   _____

8.   A cognitive science project weaves together three strands of research activity: theory development, empirical research, and model building. Each of these activities has far less impact in isolation from the other two. *Theory development* elaborates the set of constructs from which empirical research and model building take their impetus; the theory guides the experiment and forms the basis for the model. *Empirical research* validates and constrains the theory and determines the parameters of the working model. *Model building* instantiates and extends the theory and generates new hypotheses that need to be tested empirically.

—Jon M. Slack   8.   _____

80. BEYOND THE SENTENCE: PARAGRAPH DEVELOPMENT WITH SPECIFICS

(Study B-1.)

Underline the **topic sentence** of each paragraph. In addition,

write **1** in the blank at the end if the paragraph develops its topic sentence adequately **and** then write another sentence that would continue its development;
write **0** if the paragraph is not adequately developed **and** then write the reason why you think so.

1.   Young people today see how their parents feel and act. Since they feel that their parents are wrong, they rebel because they do not want to become carbon copies of their elders. Young people want to be treated as people, not just children who do not know what they are talking about and who should therefore not express their own ideas. Young people today want to do and think as they please. They do not want their ideas to be pushed aside for an older person's ideas. They want a free society where there is nothing that they must do because it is required of them. They want to experience new and different things. Whatever their elders want, they do the opposite so as not to be like them.   1. _____

2.   Today's athletes are overpaid. Although it is undeniable that not everyone can toss a basketball through a hoop or throw a baseball ninety miles an hour, that doesn't mean that fans should have to pay the admission prices they do. People who like sports have other ways to spend their money, such as movies or vacations. Some of them can't even afford to go to sporting events. Doctors and nurses also perform valuable services to society; should they be rich enough to retire at thirty-five? The cost of living for the average person continues to climb. Athletes should not be millionaires, no matter how talented they are.   2. _____

3.   Why should we turn to systems theory when addressing education? Because learning is a complex interplay of students, teachers, and subject matter. One kind of student might need a clearly defined sequence of steps while a second might prefer to jump in anywhere. One subject will call for lots of graphics; another will require close reading of language.   3. _____

4.   The study found that collection crews spent only a small portion of their day picking up garbage. Crews observed in Laval spent an average of two hours and 55 minutes at it, while those in Brossard collected garbage for three hours and 22 minutes a day, and crews in Rosemount worked on collection for three hours and 33 minutes a day.   4. _____

5.   I like the old movies shown on TV better than the ones shown in theaters in recent years. The old films contain plots that are more dramatic and actors that are more famous. Such films are exciting and fast-paced. The actors are widely known for their acting ability. Today's films often drag and have less famous actors.   5. _____

81. BEYOND THE SENTENCE: PARAGRAPH UNITY

(Study B-1.)

Underline the **topic sentence** of each paragraph. Then, in the blanks at the end of the paragraph, write the number(s) of any sentence(s) in the paragraph that **do not relate directly** to the topic sentence.

1.　^{1}From a pebble on the shore to a boulder on a mountainside, any rock you see began as something else and was made a rock by the earth itself. ^{2}Igneous rock began as lava that over hundreds of years hardened far beneath the earth's surface. ^{3}Granite is an igneous rock. ^{4}Sedimentary rock was once sand, mud, or clay that settled to the bottom of a body of water and was packed down in layers under the ocean floor. ^{5}All rocks are made up of one or more minerals. ^{6}Metamorphic rock began as either igneous rock or sedimentary rock whose properties were changed by millions of years of exposure to the heat, pressure, and movement below the earth's crust.

1. _____
　_____

2.　^{1}Although we normally associate suits of armor with the knights of medieval Europe, the idea of such protective coverings is much older and more pervasive than that. ^{2}Some knights even outfitted their horses with metal armor. ^{3}As long as 3500 years ago, Assyrian and Babylonian warriors sewed pieces of metal to their leather tunics the better to repel enemy arrows. ^{4}A thousand years later, the Greeks wore metal helmets, in addition to large metal sheets over their chests and backs. ^{5}Native Americans of the Northwest wore both carved wooden helmets and chest armor made from wood and leather. ^{6}Nature protects the turtle and the armadillo with permanent armor. ^{7}Even with body armor largely absent from the modern soldier's uniform, the helmet still remains as a reminder of the vulnerability of the human body.

2. _____
　_____

3.　^{1}Computers have forever changed the way we work. ^{2}Clerks no longer add rows of numbers by hand. ^{3}Writers are freed of keeping pages and pages of documentation on their shelves. ^{4}Many persons fear that computers will take away jobs. ^{5}Computer-controlled robots have changed the way factories manufacture everything from cars to toys. ^{6}There is always the danger of misusing the computer, such as by storing personal information about people. ^{7}Someone has even programmed a computer to flip hamburgers.

3. _____
　_____

4.　^{1}I'd much rather read a book than see a movie. ^{2}When you read, you can imagine for yourself what characters look like and how they sound. ^{3}You can pick up a book at any time and not have to line up for a film to begin. ^{4}It is true, however, that you can do the same with videos. ^{5}A book goes with you to be read anywhere—you never have to be in a specific place. ^{6}When you find a passage you like, you can reread it or just pause and think about things. ^{7}Of course, it's always fun to be in a theater with other people.

4. _____
　_____

82. BEYOND THE SENTENCE: PARAGRAPH COHERENCE—TRANSITIONS

(Study B-1.)

For each item, choose from the list the **transitional expression** that fits most logically in the space. Then write the number of that expression (**1** to **10**) in the blank at the right. (For some items there is more than one possible answer.)

1. afterward
2. consequently
3. even so
4. formerly
5. however
6. meanwhile
7. nevertheless
8. on the other hand
9. that is
10. therefore

Example: I think, _____, I am.   __10__

1. The night of the prom, we danced every step we knew. _____, we strolled on the moonlit beach.   1. _____

2. There is widespread agreement that females can do virtually any job. _____, there are still many questions about the effect this may have on the relationships between men and women.   2. _____

3. For many years, the railroad was Canada's most important means of travel. _____, with the advent of airplanes and private cars, fewer and fewer people chose to use it.   3. _____

4. I am terminating my periodic disbursement to you. _____, I am cutting off your allowance.   4. _____

5. As the nobles bickered among themselves as to who should station themselves at defensive positions and who should counterattack, the king spent increasingly more time with his astrologers. _____, the rebels marched closer to the capital.   5. _____

6. A person speaking to members of his or her own family uses language that is informal and intimate. A person speaking to a large group, _____, is likely to choose different words and a different tone of voice.   6. _____

7. If you toss a coin repeatedly and it comes up heads each time, common sense tells you to expect tails to turn up soon. _____, the chances of heads coming up remain the same for each toss of the coin.   7. _____

8. Today, computers are inexpensive enough to put in virtually every office and in every school. _____, the cost of such machines was prohibitive.   8. _____

9. In general, a small animal acclimatizes better than a large one. _____, the small animal finds it easier to adjust to changes in the environment.   9. _____

10. It was evident to the foreperson and to the other jurors that they were hopelessly deadlocked. _____, the foreperson sent word to the judge that they were unable to agree on a verdict.   10. _____

83. BEYOND THE SENTENCE: BIBLIOGRAPHIC FORM

(Open-Book Exercise—Study B-3.)

Write **1** if the entire entry is **correct** in form.
Write **0** if the entry contains any error in form (including punctuation). Circle the error.
(For this exercise, use the MLA style.)

Example: Clift, Dominique. The Secret Kingdom: Interpretations of the Canadian Character. 1989.
McClelland & Stewart, Toronto.   0

1. Book	Bercuson, David J., and Granatstein, J. L. The Collins Dictionary of Canadian History. Toronto: Collins, 1988.	1. _____
2. Book	Linda Hutcheon. The Canadian Postmodern. Toronto: Oxford University Press, 1988.	2. _____
3. Newspaper article	Lepage, Mark. "Mega-stars, Mega-bucks, and MTV." Montreal Gazette Dec. 21 1989, Fi.	3. _____
4. Article in a collection	Foucault, Michel; "What Is an Author?" Textual Strategies: Perspectives in Post-Structuralist Criticism. Ed. J. V. Harari. Ithaca: Cornell University Press, 1979.	4. _____
5. Encyclopedia article	National Hockey League. "The Canadian Encyclopedia." 1988 ed.	5. _____
6. Journal article	Pritchard, Allan. "West of the Great Divide: Man and Nature in the Literature of British Columbia." Canadian Literature 102(1984): 36–53.	6. _____
7. Magazine article	Jackson, Marni. "Bringing Up Baby." Saturday Night 104 Dec. 1989: 30–39.	7. _____
8. Magazine article	Page, Jake. "Inside the Sacred Hopi Homeland." National Geographic (162: 1982, 607–629).	8. _____
9. Journal article	Bibeau, Gilles. "No Easy Road to Bilingualism." "Language and Society" 8 (1988): 44–45.	9. _____
10. Book	Horvath, Polly. An Occasional Cow. Harper Collins, Toronto: 1989.	10. _____

84. ACHIEVEMENT TEST: GRAMMAR

Sentences

Write **1** if the boldface expression is **one complete sentence.**
Write **2** if it is a **fragment.**
Write **3** if it is a **comma splice** or **fused sentence** (run-on).

Example: *Having completely slipped its moorings.*   2

1. He decided not to go. *After buying the tickets and packing his bags.*   1. _____

2. I was urged to do two things. *To drop out of college and to go to work.*   2. _____

3. *He will attend college, his high-school grades are good enough.*   3. _____

4. First she picked up the ax. *Then she began chopping firewood.*   4. _____

5. *When I discovered a large bear staring at me.*   5. _____

6. *An hour before the concert started.* The director became ill.   6. _____

7. *Our guests having arrived, we sat down to dinner.*   7. _____

8. I visited the campus. *First I toured the library, then I went to the gymnasium.*   8. _____

9. *The storm having washed out the bridge.* We had to spend the night in town.   9. _____

10. Sir Thisby invited me to play cricket. *A game I had never even watched.*   10. _____

Grammar

Write **1** if the boldface expression is used **correctly.**
Write **0** if it is used **incorrectly.**

Example: There *was* laughing, singing, and shouting coming from the dorm.   0

1. The dean said *that* if she could help us *that* she would be glad to see us.   1. _____

2. During the summer she trained horses, *which* assisted her financially.   2. _____

3. In the room *were* an instructor, three students, and a faculty adviser.   3. _____

4. Cousin Max, along with his twin daughters and their cats, *were* waiting at my front door.   4. _____

5. The conductor asked each of the musicians to mark *their* score.   5. _____

6. A copy of *Owl* and a copy of *Chickadee was* in Dr. Moore's waiting room.   6. _____

7. Did you happen to see Tony and *I* at the theater?   7. _____

8. The ticket agent gave Ed and *I* seats that were behind home plate.   8. _____

9. Every committee member *was* given a copy of the report.   9. _____

10. *Wandering around town,* my ideas for the new play began to take shape.   10. _____

11. Parking restrictions apply *not only* to students *but also* to visitors.   11. _____

12. His mother hoped for him to be a corporation lawyer. *This* kept Leonard in college.   12. _____

13. He tried to *promptly and efficiently* complete each task assigned to him.   13. _____

14. All of *we* students protested the new attendance regulation.   14. _____

15. *Having more than an hour to kill,* there was time to stroll through the village.   15. _____

16. His plans were *joining the Foreign Legion* and *to leave school.*   16. _____

17. *Being 265 years old,* it seemed a sacrilege to cut down the giant pine.   17. _____

18. I like *swimming* and *to relax* in the warm sunshine.   18. _____

19. We wondered why the list of courses *was* not posted yet.   19. _____

20. There are few people I respect as much as *her.*   20. _____

21. *Is* either of the two bands ready to go on?   21. _____

22. *Who* did you see at the game last night?   22. _____

23. No one who plays a lottery really believes that *their* ticket will win.   23. _____

24. Aggression *is when* one nation attacks another without provocation.   24. _____

25. The dress material felt *differently* after it had been washed and ironed.   25. _____

26. Financial aid will be made available to *whoever* shows a need for it.   26. _____

27. My reason for working last summer was *that* I wanted to buy a car.   27. _____

28. He coached minor hockey and joined two service clubs. *It* was expected of him by his associates.   28. _____

29. Fritz and *myself* followed the tall, mysterious stranger.   29. _____

30. *Who* do you think will be candidates for the office of student-body president?   30. _____

31. Neither Joan nor her two attendants *was* asked to appear on television.   31. _____

32. There *was* at least eight persons involved in the traffic accident.   32. _____

33. Between you and *I,* she has very little interest in getting a European scholarship.   33. _____

34. *Is* there any objections to your opening a new store in the neighborhood?   34. _____

35. She is one of six applicants who *are* to be interviewed tomorrow.   35. _____

36. Are you sure that it was *they* whom you saw in the post office?   36. _____

37. My boyfriend suggested I take Russian. *That* was fine with me.   37. _____

38. You will never find anyone more responsible than *her.*   38. _____

39. Jane is the *friendliest* of the two sisters.   39. _____

40. Paul cooks *like* he were a professional chef.   40. _____

41. Each of the players *has* two passes for all home games.   41. _____

42. Why not give the keys to *whomever* you think will be in charge?   42. _____

43. Do you approve of *his* going away to college?   43. _____

44. Several of *we* students had decided to start a petition addressed to the deans.   44. _____

45. On the bench *were* a book, a coat, and an umbrella.   45. _____

46. The coach, as well as the manager and the players, *was* confident of winning.   46. _____

47. *Knowing of her parents' disapproval,* it seemed wise for her to reconsider her plan.   47. _____

48. He had decided to *only* spend two dollars for a gift.   48. _____

49. If he *were* more tactful, he would have fewer enemies.   49. _____

50. Lena chose Dominic and *I* to be her audience.   50. _____

51. Neither the camp director nor the hikers *was* aware of their danger.   51. _____

52. He purchased the only one of the books that *was* of any value to him.   52. _____

53. She suggested that Lucille and *I* attend the opening lecture. 53. _____

54. He told Steve and *I* to try to sell tickets at the dance. 54. _____

55. My friends and *myself* enjoyed our skiing trip. 55. _____

56. Each of the players *gives* a convincing performance. 56. _____

57. The poor writing and the sloppiness of the research *forces* me to fail your essay. 57. _____

58. *Shouting loudly,* Josh's noise was unbearable. 58. _____

59. I hate spinach even though it gives *you* muscles. 59. _____

60. When the Canucks and the Oilers play, I know *they* will win. 60. _____

85. ACHIEVEMENT TEST: PUNCTUATION

Write **1** if the punctuation in brackets is **correct.**
Write **0** if it is **incorrect.**
(Use only one number in each blank.)

Example: Stuart took lessons in using[,] word processing, data base, and spread sheet programs.　　　　　　__0__

1. Yarmouth, Nova Scotia[,] was their first stop on the trip east.　　1. _____
2. The neighbors[,] who own the barking dog[,] refuse to do anything about it.　　2. _____
3. I wanted to call on the Madisons, but I wasn't sure which house was their[']s.　　3. _____
4. Our flight having been announced[,] we hurried to board our plane.　　4. _____
5. We went for a ride in the country[. The] day being warm and balmy.　　5. _____
6. When Jules returned the book he borrowed, it[']s cover was torn.　　6. _____
7. Haven't you often heard it said, "Haste makes waste["?]　　7. _____
8. "Wouldn't you like to go to the rally with us?"[,] asked the girl across the hall.　　8. _____
9. He said, "Let's walk across the campus.["] ["]It's such a beautiful evening."　　9. _____
10. Enrollment is up to three[-]thousand students this semester.　　10. _____
11. Twenty[-]six students have volunteered to serve on various committees.　　11. _____
12. Dear Sir[;] I believe that I am just the person who can run your business more efficiently.　　12. _____
13. After you have finished your history assignment[,] shall we go to the auditorium?　　13. _____
14. Billy Budd struck Claggart[,] because he could not express himself any other way.　　14. _____
15. This is the color you ordered[,] isn't it?　　15. _____
16. We were early[;] as a matter of fact, we were the first of the guests to arrive.　　16. _____
17. "If you are really serious about your work," the instructor said[,] "you'll succeed."　　17. _____
18. Dr. Johnson had little praise for patriotism[;] calling it the last refuge of a scoundrel.　　18. _____
19. The band recorded its first album in the spring[,] and followed it with a concert tour in the summer.　　19. _____
20. She had hoped to arrange a two month[']s tour of the Orient.　　20. _____
21. This is your office[,] Ms. Foster; I trust that it will be satisfactory.　　21. _____
22. The next eclipse will take place July 26, 1992[,] but will be visible only in the Maritimes.　　22. _____
23. All the cars[,] which were without new licenses[,] were being stopped by the police.　　23. _____
24. Because she had watched television until after midnight[;] she overslept.　　24. _____
25. A medal was awarded to Jane Cox, a high-school student[,] for rescuing the children.　　25. _____
26. Professor Thomas agreed to direct a play for the Childrens['] Theater.　　26. _____
27. The boy at the left of the picture[,] would become a bank robber in later life.　　27. _____
28. "As for who has written the winning essay[—]well, I haven't as yet heard from the judges," said Mr. Hawkins.　　28. _____
29. What he described about the massive oil spill in Alaska[,] filled us with horror.　　29. _____
30. I asked Elizabeth what we should do about plane reservations[?]　　30. _____

31. The newly elected officers are Kenneth Chamberlin, president[;] Ruby Pillsbury, vice-president[;] and Mildred Levy, secretary-treasurer. 31. _____

32. Many weeks before school was over[;] she was planning a vacation trip. 32. _____

33. We followed the trail over several ridges[,] and along the edges of two mountain lakes. 33. _____

34. Before going to Europe, I had many matters to attend to[;] such as making reservations, buying clothes, and getting a passport. 34. _____

35. Having a good sense of humor helps you put things in perspective[;] certainly, it's better than brooding. 35. _____

36. The ticket agent inquired ["]if we were planning to stop in Paris.["] 36. _____

37. The Girls' Club sold cookies[;] planned a camping trip[;] and worked for the YWCA. 37. _____

38. Marcia learned that all foods[,] which are high in calories[,] were to be avoided. 38. _____

39. We were told to read ["]Ode to a Nightingale,["] a poem by Keats. 39. _____

40. The alumni magazine had a column cleverly entitled ["]Grad-Tidings.["] 40. _____

41. She had told the maid to bring[:] pillowcases, sheets, and a mattress pad. 41. _____

42. Some people still wish to have ["]The Maple Leaf Forever["] become our national anthem. 42. _____

43. She hurried toward us[,] her books clasped under her arm[,] to tell us the good news. 43. _____

44. The audience wanted him to sing one more song[;] however, he refused. 44. _____

45. The enthusiastic response of his audience[;] however, made him change his mind. 45. _____

46. She found a note in her mailbox: "Sorry to have missed you. The Lawson[']s." 46. _____

47. His father wanted him to major in engineering[;] he wanted to major in music. 47. _____

48. Chris decided he wanted to be an unemployed poet[;] not a well-paid engineer. 48. _____

49. He had gone to the library[. B]ecause he needed more material for his term paper. 49. _____

50. Her program included courses in English[,] social science[,] and chemistry. 50. _____

51. The two women, not having very much in common[;] found very little to say to each other. 51. _____

52. To be able to speak confidently before a group[;] Donna enrolled in a speech class. 52. _____

53. Ms. Whitney, who is the gym teacher, came to the rally[;] and Mr. Martin, who is the football coach, introduced the players. 53. _____

54. By working in a grocery store after school[,] Lloyd was able to save money for college. 54. _____

55. "Some of the seniors wer[']ent able to pay their dues," she said. 55. _____

56. Frank Anderson[,] who is on the debating team[,] is an excellent speaker. 56. _____

57. "All motorists[,] who fail to stop at a crosswalk[,] should be put in jail!" said one parent. 57. _____

58. Looking at me sweetly, Mark replied, "No[,] there is no way in the world I'd ever marry you." 58. _____

59. George enrolled in a course in home economics; Elsa[,] in a course in woodworking. 59. _____

60. "Haven't I met you somewhere before?"[,] he asked. 60. _____

61. "It's most unlikely!"[,] she said, turning away. 61. _____

62. Joe Ackerman, a man[,] whom I had met in the service, called to see me. 62. _____

63. Mother placed the note about dinner[,] where she knew the family would see it. 63. _____

64. He moved to Windsor[,] where he attended the university. 64. _____

65. We were[,] on the other hand[,] not surprised at his decision. 65. _____

66. Knowing that her cousins would be waiting for her at the airport[;] Imogene walked briskly toward the gate.   66. _____

67. Listen to the arguments of both speakers[,] then decide which side you favor.   67. _____

86. ACHIEVEMENT TEST: MECHANICS, SPELLING, USAGE

Capitalization

Write **1** if the boldface word(s) **follow** the rules of capitalization.
Write **0** if they **do not.**

Example: Uncle Spike is a **Shortstop.** _0_
Their shortstop is **Uncle Spike.** _1_

1. I barely passed **spanish.** 1. _____
2. My brother attends **High School.** 2. _____
3. He is **President** of his company. 3. _____
4. Janet is the club **treasurer.** 4. _____
5. I belong to the **Science Club.** 5. _____
6. He plays for **Montreal West.** 6. _____
7. We saluted the **canadian** flag. 7. _____
8. My **Uncle** plays shortstop. 8. _____
9. I told **Grandfather** that he was being very kind to me. 9. _____
10. He likes living in the **North.** 10. _____
11. I shall go east next **Spring.** 11. _____
12. She enrolled in **History 101.** 12. _____

13. I visited an **indian** village near Bombay. 13. _____
14. Arthur is now in **college.** 14. _____
15. Emily attends a **University.** 15. _____
16. He enjoys his **history** course. 16. _____
17. The Ottawa **river** overflowed. 17. _____
18. Fetch; **Sit.** 18. _____
19. "You are," **he** said, "the one." 19. _____
20. I ended it with "Yours **Sincerely."** 20. _____
21. "What," he asked, **"Is** wrong?" 21. _____
22. We met on **New Year's Eve.** 22. _____
23. The show opens **Monday.** 23. _____
24. The note began, "My **Dear** John." 24. _____
25. I'm going to be a **Star.** 25. _____

Abbreviations and Numbers

Write **1** if the boldface abbreviation or number is used **correctly.**
Write **0** if it is used **incorrectly.**

Example: **2's** company, three's a crowd. _0_

1. This is her **20th** birthday. 1. _____
2. Thank God it's **Fri.** 2. _____
3. My dog Spot is **3.** 3. _____
4. I saw him on Mission **St.** today. 4. _____
5. She was born on July **6th,** 1964. 5. _____
6. Please met me at **10 o'clock.** 6. _____
7. He released **two hundred** red balloons at the dance. 7. _____

8. The train leaves at **8 P.M.** 8. _____
9. Dinner was served at **six o'clock.** 9. _____
10. Joan Allen, **Ph.D.,** spoke first. 10. _____
11. Lunch cost **6** dollars. 11. _____
12. **Ms.** Horvath, take a letter. 12. _____
13. Harry Brown's monthly salary is now **$565.50.** 13. _____
14. The Fox **Co.** is selling out. 14. _____
15. We learned that **14** students received scholarship awards. 15. _____

Spelling

In each sentence, **one** boldface word is **misspelled**; write its number in the blank.

Example: (1)*Their* (2)*questionnaries* have been (3)*received.*   ___2___

1. (1)*It's* (2)*unusual* for him to be so (3)*conscientous,* isn't it?   1. _____
2. The closed (1)*cemetary* gates presented a (2)*dilemma* to Karloff's (3)*laboratory* assistant.   2. _____
3. Does the (1)*psychology* (2)*proffesor* require (3)*written* assignments?   3. _____
4. I (1)*believe* that he will do well in (2)*competition* with other (3)*atheletes.*   4. _____
5. The (1)*sophomore* student learned that a (2)*knowledge* of (3)*grammer* is helpful.   5. _____
6. A (1)*fourth* such disaster threatens the very (2)*existance* of the Alaskan (3)*environment.*   6. _____
7. He considers that it's (1)*definately* a (2)*privilege* to live in this (3)*environment.*   7. _____
8. The (1)*principal* (2)*complimented* her for her (3)*excellant* performance.   8. _____
9. It was (1)*apparent* that she had (2)*profitted* by listening to his (3)*advice.*   9. _____
10. Isn't it (1)*occasionally* (2)*desirable* to engage in a lively (3)*arguement*?   10. _____
11. Is it (1)*permissable* to ask him to (2)*recommend* me for a (3)*government* position?   11. _____
12. He showed a (1)*tendency* to (2)*reminisce* about his early (3)*achievments.*   12. _____
13. The test pilot felt enormous (1)*exhileration* after his third (2)*repetition* of the dangerous (3)*maneuver.*   13. _____
14. It's (1)*conceivable* that the (2)*omission* might prove to be (3)*disasterous.*   14. _____
15. He was not (1)*conscious* of being (2)*unnecessarily* (3)*persistant* about the matter.   15. _____

Usage

Write **1** if the boldface expression is used **correctly.**
Write **0** if it is used **incorrectly.**

Example: In *actual fact,* Karin was there.   ___0___

1. I was not *altogether* amused.   1. _____
2. Rover looks *sort of* sick.   2. _____
3. They are all old; for *instants,* Grayson is eighty-six.   3. _____
4. Billy cried when his balloon *burst.*   4. _____
5. Try to make *fewer* mistakes.   5. _____
6. He earned no interest on his *principal.*   6. _____
7. *Can* I add your name to the list?   7. _____
8. The judge would hear no *farther* arguments.   8. _____
9. I'm in real trouble, *aren't I?*   9. _____
10. We were *plenty* angry.   10. _____

11. I *rarely ever* hear from her.   11. _____
12. He notified *most* of his creditors.   12. _____
13. She has *less* excuses than I.   13. _____
14. Saul made an *illusion* to *Hamlet.*   14. _____
15. Was the killer *hanged*?   15. _____
16. Eleanor feels *some* better now.   16. _____
17. Her ideas were different *from* mine.   17. _____
18. I had *already* signed the check.   18. _____
19. Jay sounds *like* he's serious this time.   19. _____
20. I dislike *those kind* of promises.   20. _____
21. He became *real* independent.   21. _____
22. The dog is *lying* by the fire.   22. _____

23. She **generally always** works hard.

24. He does **good** in math courses.

23. _____

24. _____

25. His speech **implied** that he would raise taxes.

25. _____

87. ACHIEVEMENT TEST: DOCUMENTATION

(Open-Book Test)

Write **1** for each statement that is **true**.
Write **0** for each that is **false**.
(For this exercise, use the MLA style.)

1. The titles of all books are underlined to designate *italics*.   1. _____

2. A *semicolon* is used to separate the place of the publication from the name of the publisher.   2. _____

3. Some of the author's words in a direct quotation may be omitted provided that you indicate the omission by the use of *three periods*.   3. _____

4. The titles of all magazine articles are underlined to show *italics*.   4. _____

5. The author's *last* name is the first item in a *bibliographic entry*.   5. _____

6. The title of each magazine is enclosed in *quotation marks*.   6. _____

7. The terminal punctuation of each bibliographic entry is a *period*.   7. _____

8. A *bibliographic entry for a journal article* includes just author's name, title of magazine, volume number, date, and pages covered.   8. _____

9. If you insert a word (or words) of your own in a direct quotation, enclose this insertion in *parentheses*.   9. _____

10. The word *encyclopedia* is spelled differently in the titles of the two publications *Encyclopaedia Britannica* and *The Canadian Encyclopedia*.   10. _____

11. If a *misspelled word* exists in the statement that you are quoting, copy it and follow it with the word *sic* enclosed in brackets.   11. _____

12. The title of a television program should be underlined to show *italics*.   12. _____

13. The title of an article in an encyclopedia should be underlined to show *italics*.   13. _____

14. If a book is written by *three authors,* the names of all three should be listed in a bibliographic entry.   14. _____

15. A *comma* follows the author's full name in a bibliographic entry for a book having one author.   15. _____

16. A citation such as (*Smith 381*) in *parentheses* in your text may be used instead of a footnote.   16. _____

17. The title of a bulletin published by the Canadian Government is enclosed in *quotation marks*.   17. _____

18. The abbreviation *et al.* may be used to indicate "and others" if a publication has *more than three* authors.   18. _____

19. A *number* should precede each entry in a bibliography.   19. _____

20. A *period* follows the title of a book in a bibliographic entry.   20. _____

21. A *period* follows the last name of a single author in a bibliographic entry.   21. _____

22. The title of a newspaper is enclosed in *quotation marks*.   22. _____

23. If a magazine article is *unsigned*, the first item in a bibliographic entry is the *title of the article*.   23. _____

24. The last item in a *bibliographic entry for a magazine article* is the page number (or numbers) on which the article appears.   24. _____

25. The title of an essay in a collection is underlined to show *italics*.   25. _____

Write **1** for each bibliographic entry that is **correct** in form.
Write **0** for each that is **incorrect.**
(For this exercise, use the MLA style.)

1. **Book**   Richler, Mordechai. <u>Solomon Gursky Was Here.</u>   Toronto: Viking, 1989.   **1.** _____

2. **Book**   O'Shea, Tim, and Marc Eisenstadt. <u>Artificial Intelligence: Tools,</u>   **2.** _____
   <u>Techniques, and Applications.</u>   New York; Harper & Row, 1984.

3. **Encyclopedia article**   Morris, Leonard.   "Gold Rush."   <u>The Canadian Encyclopedia</u> (1989 ed.), II;   **3.** _____
   31–32.

4. **Magazine article**   Thompson, Tom.   "Full-Spectrum Scanners."   <u>"Byte,"</u> (April 1989), 189–194.   **4.** _____

5. **Newspaper article (unsigned)**   "Oilers Win in Overtime."   <u>Edmonton Journal.</u>   23 Dec. 1989: B6.   **5.** _____

6. **Essay or article in a collection**   Greenblatt, Stephen.   "Invisible Bullets: Renaissance Authority and Its Subver-   **6.** _____
   sion."   <u>Political Shakespeare: New Essays in Cultural Materialism.</u>
   Ed. Jonathan Dollimore and Alan Sinfield.   Manchester: Manchester University Press, 1985. 18–47.

A List of Grammatical Terms

The following chart gives brief definitions, examples, and nonexamples of the grammatical terms you'll read about most often in these exercises. Refer to *English Simplified* for more information.

Term	What It *Is* or *Does*	Examples	Nonexamples
Adjective	Describes a noun.	a *fast* runner (describes the noun *runner*)	He runs *fast.* (describes the verb runs)
Adverb	Describes a verb, adjective, or another adverb.	He runs *fast.* (describes the verb *run*) He is an *extremely* fast runner. (describes the adjective *fast*) He runs *very* fast. (describes the adverb *fast*)	He is a *fast* runner. (Here, *fast* is an adjective.)
Appositive	A noun that renames another.	Tom Wolfe, *the writer,* lives in New York. (The appositive follows the man's name.)	*Tom Wolfe,* the writer, lives in New York.
Clause	A group of words with a subject and a predicate. A *main clause* can stand by itself and make complete sense; a *dependent clause* must be attached to a main clause.	*He is a fast runner.* (a main clause) *if he is a fast runner* (a dependent clause that must be attached to some main clause; for example, *he would win*)	a *fast runner* (merely a noun and its adjective)
Complement	Completes the meaning of the verb.	Direct object: He threw the *ball.* (says what got thrown) Indirect object: He threw the ball to *me.* (says who benefited by the ball being thrown) Subjective complement: He is a *pitcher.* (renames the subject *He* after the linking verb *is*) Objective complement: The team named Rodgers *coach.* (follows the direct object *Rodgers* and renames it)	*He* threw the ball. (says who did the action rather than received it)
Conjunction	A word that joins.	Coordinating conjunction: Joins things of equal importance: boys *and* girls; poor *but* honest. Subordinating conjunction: Joins a dependent clause to a main clause: I left *when* she arrived.	I left *at* noon. (*At* is a preposition.)
Fragment	A group of words that cannot stand by themselves and make complete sense.	*when I saw them* (a dependent clause) *from Maine to California* (a prepositional phrase)	*They went from Maine to California.* (a main clause that can stand by itself)

Term	What It *Is* or *Does*	Examples	Nonexamples
Noun	Names a person, place, animal, or thing.	*Tom, Denver, cat, book*	*throw* (a verb) *red* (an adjective)
Phrase	A group of words without both a subject and a verb.	*from California* (a prepositional phrase) *to see the king* (an infinitive phrase) *built of bricks* (a participial phrase) *building houses* (a gerund phrase)	*He is from California.* (a main clause)
Predicate	The part of the sentence that speaks about the subject.	The man *threw the ball.* (says what the subject did)	The *man* threw the ball. (The *man* performed the action.)
Pronoun	A word that replaces a noun.	*He* will be here soon. (*He* takes the place of the man's name.)	*Jonathan* will be here soon. (*Jonathan* is a proper noun.)
Subject	The person or thing about whom the sentence speaks.	*Polly* writes children's books.	Polly *writes children's books.* (*Writes children's books* is the predicate, that is, the action she performs.)
Verb	Says what the subject either *does* or *is*.	She *buys* seashells. She *is* smart.	*Emily* is smart. (*Emily* is a noun.)

DIAGRAMING

Diagraming is a method of analyzing sentences and of visually depicting parts of speech and their functions in sentences. Though diagrams can grow complex, their basic principle is simple: Everything in the complete subject is written to the left of the main vertical line; everything in the complete predicate, to the right. All the main parts of a sentence are written on or above the main horizontal line; all the secondary parts, below the main horizontal line.

Simple sentence

An old friend from school often sends me very funny postcards.

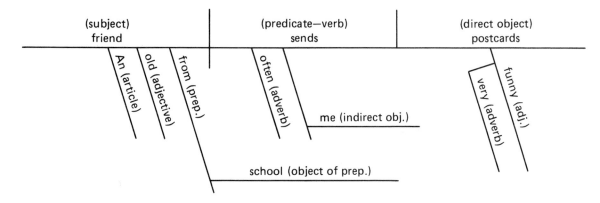

Simple sentence with compound parts

Romeo and Juliet fell in love and planned a secret wedding.

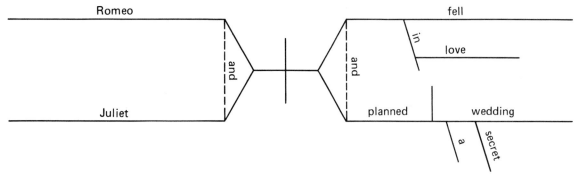

Verbals and verbal phrases

Used as modifiers

Reeling under our attacks (participial phrase), the *decimated* (participle) enemy requested a truce *to arrange a surrender* (infinitive phrase).

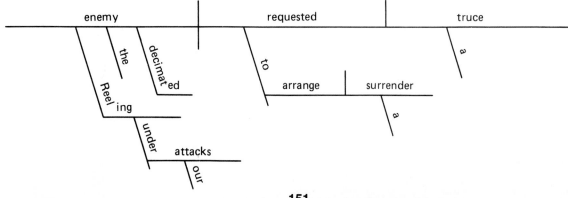

151

Verbals and verbal phrases

Used as nouns

They denied *having tried to embezzle funds by falsifying data.* (Italicized words are a gerund phrase; within that phrase are an infinitive phrase, *to embezzle funds*, and another gerund phrase, *falsifying data.)*

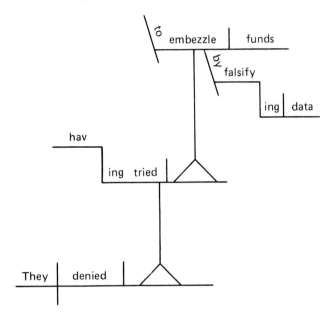

Compound sentence

We tried hard, but we failed badly.

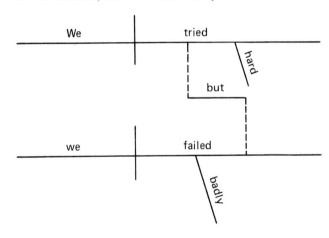

Complex sentence

With adjective clause (dotted line between relative pronoun and antecedent)

I respect a person *who can resist pressure.*

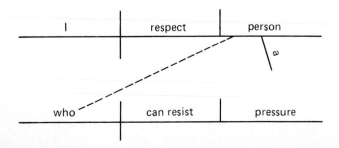

Complex sentence

With adverb clause (dotted line between verb of adverb clause and word the clause modifies)

We will continue our campaign *until we make Jones mayor.*

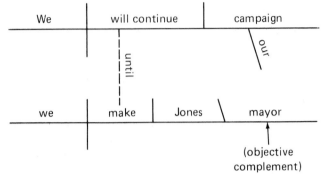

With noun clause (on tower)

You should take *whatever you can get.*

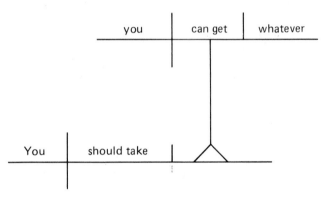

That you will succeed is almost certain.

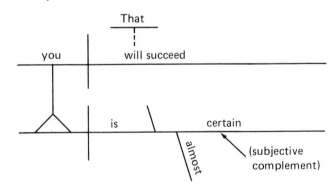

Give it to *whoever answers the door.*

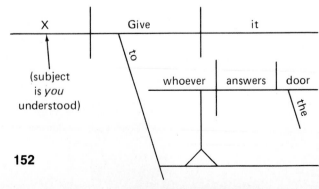

152